Lori s Song

The true story of an American woman held captive in Iran

by Lori Foroozandeh

Outskirts Press, Inc.
Denver, Colorado

Lori's Song
The true story of an American woman held captive in Iran

Outskirts Press, Inc.
http://www.outskirtspress.com

ISBN: 978-1-4327-3829-7 Paperback
ISBN: 978-1-4327-1182-5 Hardback

Library of Congress Control Number: 2009927886

Outskirts Press and the "OP" logo are trademarks belonging to Outskirts Press, Inc.

PRINTED IN THE UNITED STATES OF AMERICA

AUTHOR'S NOTE

When I first started writing this book in 2002 I didn't want to make it a story about mudslinging. I didn't want to make my parents look bad, or write about why I divorced the first two times (due to my sister sleeping with my husbands). This book was only supposed to be about Iran. But as I was told later after the book was finished; it was unfair to only make myself out to be the bad person. Many of us who are abused either sexually or physically always try to somehow make it out to be OUR FAULT! That is why rather than change the first chapter I would like to include it the way it is. Maybe society can get a good look at the depth of how someone like "us" will go to extreme lengths to protect those that abuse us the most!

And I would also like to add that after going through 6 years of on and off therapy I have finally found a doctor (neurologist) and therapist who both specialize in the disorder of PTSD; I.e. Post traumatic stress disorder. I met these two in 2006 and they have helped me realize that I can trust again and possibly even deal with all of my issues. I trust these two with my life and they are the reason that this book is finally being published today.

I would also like to add and emphasize that I did start writing this book in 2002 since everyone told me that it would be a catharsis for my sadness and frustration.

No one was ever contacted for publicity on this book so it was not for sensationalism that is was written. Also with the sales of this book I will be making donations to the organizations that have helped me in dealing with my drug addiction, my PTSD, and to Amnesty International to help those women who aren't able to escape the horrors of their own country to hopefully one day enjoy the freedom that the USA offers! Now on with my early beginnings and what got me here in the first place!

FOREWORD

I was adopted at 6 months old into a family of two sisters and one brother. My foster parents that adopted me told me that I had been taken away from my birth parents due to being severely abused by them. They told me that when the state brought me, I had cigarette burns all over my body, and that I hadn't had a bath in weeks. That my diaper pins actually had rust on them. Apparently, I had been kept in a closet for the first six months of my life and only fed milk. Therefore, I got off to a rough start in life. That is only the half of it. I grew up in a family where I was the only adopted child. My two sisters, whom were 11 years and 9 years older than me, and my brother who was 8 years older were all somewhat jealous of me. I guess the reasoning was that I was now the "baby" of the family; and came along at a time when our parents had more money so they were able to buy more things while I was growing up. My mother still favored my brother because she let him, get away with some awful acts…. Mostly against me.

The most memorable one was when I was age 10. He started playing this game called "tickle". It began with an agreement that if he tickled my foot while watching TV, then I would tickle his foot in return. This was fine since it was relaxing. Then it became more ….my bedroom was in our basement as was all of us kids bedrooms. The basement had been finished so that there was a poolroom (Pool table room) and my brother's bed was there, since he was 18 and still living at home, as were my two sisters who kept beds downstairs as well. Now that I think back, the game might have actually started much earlier than 10 years old, because I remember my sisters yelling at my brother when he would insist that I "tickle" him, because they had to get up early to go to school. I say I cannot remember well when it started because it really is not the type of thing that you WANT TO REMEMBER….that is your brother using a game of tickle to molest you!

The first time it happened, he crawled in my bed and rather than asking me to play tickle, he TOLD me that WE WERE GOING TO PLAY! I just said ok not thinking anything was odd, and then he grabbed my hand and wanted me to tickle an area that was not his foot. I jerked away and told him that was not his foot. He then told me that when you play in bed you do not tickle each other's feet. I told him that I did not want to play because I was tired. He told me that if we DIDN'T he would tell our mom and she would ground me. My sisters were downstairs and within hearing distance so I believed what he was saying to be true. Therefore, I reluctantly did what he told me to do.

Then he would tickle areas on me that were not my feet as well. This went on and on, and every night he would tell me that if I told mom she would get mad because she did not want to be bothered with these types of complaints, yet if I did not do it she would ground me for not listening to him. As I said my sisters were downstairs and listening, so I believed him. Moreover, my mother favored my brother so I did not want to make her angry with me.

His cruelty began then due to my resistance of his "tickle" games. He thought I should like it and want to reciprocate a little more willing than I was. He would do things: and these acts were while my mom was standing at the front door watching and laughing so this only validated his claims that she would have gotten mad had I said anything against him regarding his acts of molesting me with his "tickle" game. One time he asked me to hold the jumper cables of his motorcycle while he tried to start it. I was young and had no idea that I would be shocked when he would kick start it. As I said, my mother was standing at the front door watching and laughing as he did it. Then came the time when he called me out to the garage and had my pet bunny hanging upside down in his hand, I asked him what he was doing, he then hit it over the head and killed it! I began crying and yelling at him and his excuse was it was getting old so killing it was necessary! That night we were eating dinner and I thought we were eating chicken, until my brother informed me at the supper table that we were eating rabbit and it was mine. My mother yelled at him but never denied the fact.

After these acts of cruelty, he would always crawl into my bed at night and tell me he was sorry and was going to make everything better by just "tickling" me that night. I would yell and tell him no. He would get mad sometimes, slap me, and tell me to shut up or he would have to go and get mom. I was scared since I was convinced that she knew what was going on. How could a mother not know what was going on, after these "tickle" games started I was scared to death to be left alone in the house with him. Anytime my mom and dad had to leave to go somewhere I would start crying hysterically and beg to go with them. One time I was banging on the screen door so hard to get their attention that I ended up breaking it with my hand and cutting my hand so bad that it almost needed stitches. They still went out but only after my mom screamed at me for breaking the door.

My dad at the time had no idea what was going on, but I did not learn this until just recently in life. After my mother passed away in 2007, my father and I became close and he admitted to me that he never knew how to read or write and mom never shared anything with him. After she died, my brother took everything away from my dad including his house and any personal property he could take/steal. My mom left him everything without telling my dad. She always favored my brother and left my dad in the dark about everything. She would act as if she spoiled me for appearances sake but when there was only her, my brother and I around she allowed him to be as blatantly cruel as he wanted, without openly molesting me. She stayed in denial about that. Every time I wanted to tell her, she would get mad and tell me she did not have time to talk right then. I told my father after she died and he believed me without question.

All the while I was growing up I was a straight A student, I would win school wide spelling bees and continually make the honor roll. The school would hold banquets in my honor yet my Mother would never attend. She would always make the excuse that she did not have anyone to baby-sit; she had an adult foster care home the entire time I was growing up at home. Thus, you needed someone over the age of 18 at the house all the time. Come to find out my father was never aware of these banquets. My mother told him that I was a wild child who constantly was getting in trouble. This played in well since when I reached junior high school I had become wild since I did not care anymore and I would do anything to escape the house. I had a boyfriend whose mother would allow me to stay at their house all the time. This was wonderful because then I did not have to be around my brother who had graduated to far more than the tickle game by the time I reached 13; which I will explain later. At 15, I married just to get out of the house and escape my brother for the last time. I found a man who was the age of approx; 23 and told my mother that if she didn't allow me to get married I would get pregnant and go to Maryland where they would allow me to get married legally. At the tender age of 15, my mother signed an emancipation proclamation so that I could go to Missouri and get married... Finally, I had escaped the hell of my brother!

Now I digress back to the age of 13 or 12 not that it matters. At age 12 or 13 I lost my virginity and this was really an unfortunate event for me at home. However, this was my brothers **BIG GRADUATION** so to speak... he had been waiting for this! I came home on a Sunday night from being at my boyfriends all weekend, when my brother came over to my room (yes he was still living at home), and asked me how the week-end had went. I said fine. He then asked me if I had used condoms. I said that was none of his business, he then said he was concerned for me and that he had some if I needed them, I told him no that Tim had them when we thought we needed them. Then he smiled and said, "I KNEW IT!" I looked at him and wondered what the hell he was smiling about, he then began to tell me that now that I was no longer a virgin we could finally graduate from the tickle game. I was then terrified, and told him I was tired and that it was not right because we were brother and sister! He then began to explain that it was ok because I was adopted and mom had explained this all to him a while back. I just looked at him with disbelief at what I was hearing, but at the same time not doubting him, since my mother still allowed his bedroom to be in the basement next to mine even though she knew I had tried to tell her things and she knew how I acted when he was around.

The next thing I knew he had me on the floor and was telling me to keep my mouth shut that it wouldn't' take long and that I would enjoy it much more than I did with my pansy ass boyfriend. I just laid there and cried and he told me that the only reason I was crying was that I should have had him broken my cherry rather than Timmy...my boyfriend. These molestations went on every chance he got, until finally one night I began screaming and hitting him until I heard the basement door open. We both knew it was mom and rather than come all the way down the stairs she came half way down and just yelled at my brother and I remember her exact words: "Tell Lori Ann to keep it quiet or she will wake your Dad up!" I could not believe it, she never asked what was wrong, nor came all the way down the stairs to see if I was Ok! He just smiled and started walking towards with me with this belt in his hand, I couldn't believe what I was seeing, then he said bend over my knee because you heard mom, she said to keep you quiet, so that is what I'm supposed to do. I told him to go to hell and he grabbed me, put his hand over my mouth, and shoved me onto the bed and this was the night that ended it for a while for me, because what happened next I would never forget. He raped me and it was bad, I was bleeding and not just from the rape but from his nails that he had dug into my face trying to keep me from screaming. Afterwards I was crying so bad that I picked up the phone and was going to call Tim's mom and have her come and get me and I was going to live there until I graduated from high school. He actually looked sorry for the first time in his life. I think he even had tears in his eyes. He told me that he loved me, and I could not believe it, I about died from shock. He told me that he just wanted me to know how much he loved me and this is how he showed it. He promised me that he would never do it again. I accepted his apology. I do not know why but I felt sorry for him. He went and got a cold washcloth from upstairs and washed the blood off my face and asked me to lie down next to him so that he knew I was all right. For reasons I cannot explain, I did what he asked, and the next day I got up thinking that my life would be different with him.

The molestations ceased for a while and I actually did believe he was sorry, but then I came to find out why…he had a girlfriend! One night I came home from Tim's and my mom told me that my brother had his girlfriend over and she warned me to be nice to her. I thought this was strange since I had never had a reason to be mean to any of his girlfriends before. But then again he had never brought any of them home either. When I came inside they were both standing at the sink and he was smiling like the Cheshire cat. He introduced me to her and I was polite and then excused myself and went to my room. I was ecstatic. Finally, he had someone that would keep him away from me. She was pretty but shy. While I was downstairs, my brother came down and asked me why I was not upstairs getting to know her. I told him that I had homework to do. He insisted that I come up and talk to her. Therefore, I did. Big deal I thought a few minutes to shut him up. She was nice and polite but shy. She told me that she had heard a lot about me and that it all had been good. I just looked at her and for whatever reason got sarcastic and said well if you are going to be with him you cannot believe everything you hear. Then I walked away and went downstairs slamming the basement door. Boy was that the wrong thing to do.

That night after taking her home, he came downstairs and started yelling at me for telling her that. I was yelling back when he grabbed me and once more," had his way with me!" Only this time I just let it happen. I did not care anymore. I told him go ahead get your kicks you will anyway. He did but I do not think he enjoyed it that much so it gave me some pleasure. The next day I met Mike my husband to be. About 6 months later I was about to be married. But not until I had, been molested a few more times. Once out of the house I told him if he ever touched me again I would have Mike beat his ass. However, I never told Mike. I was too embarrassed. How could I tell the man that I was married to about sexual acts between a brother and sister? After all these were supposed to be "sick" unspoken acts. Things that only happened in "trashy" families. I could not admit to something like that. Not to mention how weak I felt for not stopping them in the first place. And for some reason my brother always had a way of making me feel like he was the only one in the world who really cared about me; when he really was the only one who despised me and degraded me in every way possible. He is responsible for the way I interact with men today. He is responsible for the way my life started on its path of destruction. Sure I can't put all the blame on him, I have to take some responsibility, but when you grow up once idolizing a brother who eventually does what he did to me, then afterwards he claims to have done it because he loved you; it leaves one totally confused and screwed up when it comes to relationships if not life in general.

My life began with him protecting me, then that protectiveness led to tickle games which I thought were for "MY BENEFIT AND PLEASURE" i.e. tickling my feet, then I became confused as to the meaning behind them. Then I was fooled into believing that I was making everyone happy by complying with him and his games because had I not complied I would have made my brother unhappy and my mother mad. Moreover, I believed these games were accepted by everyone since my sisters were in earshot and could hear what was going on.

(To this day I can only succumb to the notion that they really did not care what was going on since they were jealous of me and never liked me anyway…we still do not speak to one another). After all this, I was looking for anything that would take me far far away from the memories and horror of my childhood. Unfortunately, I found drugs. They not only numbed my feelings, but also gave me false confidence to do things that I normally would not think of doing. However, later in life I also learned that I suffered from Bi-polar that also contributed to a lot of my bad decision-making and other behavior mechanisms that were not always on the positive side.

But to make a long story short after years of drug abuse to numb the memories and many bad decisions and relationships in search of Mr. Right to protect me from Mr. Wrong (my brother), I finally found peace of mind through a drug rehabilitation place called Brighton Hospital. I have been on some substance trying to numb my feelings since age 15, but finally at age 42, I have become clean and sober thanks to Brighton Hospital and a drug called Suboxone. I am finally dealing with my mental disorder of Bi-polar that I was diagnosed with in 2005, and have been clean and for the most part pain free due to the Drug Rehabilitation Clinic at Brighton Hospital and what I call the "MIRACLE" drug Suboxone. I still suffer from PTSD, Bi-Polar, and will always suffer from drug abuse but now I do not have to suffer from its USE. I am seeing a therapist weekly and am sincerely trying to make my life a life that I can deal with without drugs. Sure, it is the hardest thing that I have ever had to do. However, with the help of God and my fiancé John, I think that I will finally succeed at living life and not just existing in it. I apologize for the sarcastic way that you might interpret my usage of my past drug use. It is in no way to make light of it. It was the only way that I could get my point of TRUTH across for the moment of time that I was trying to depict at that stage of my life.

When I originally wrote this book, I tried to tell it without mudslinging making my family look like they were the heroes and I was the black sheep. I did not want to go into all the hurt and memories of being molested nor the reasoning behind WHY I got married at 15: or WHY I was upset at not getting a bike for Christmas even though I had received a snowmobile. The reasoning here was that receiving a bike would mean that I could take trips for hours out of the house, I could ride to my boyfriends house and then call home and tell my mom that it was too dark to return home so that I had to stay there. Tim (my boyfriends mother never seemed to care when I stayed; she was the nicest woman on earth and always came to my school functions). So that bike gave me freedom from home which meant freedom from my brother, whereas that snowmobile while nice still meant supervision and that meant staying around the house. Therefore, while you read this, keep in mind I was trying hard not to delve into the details of the whole sordid chaos of my life, I was trying to tell the "main" story. However, like all good therapist, mine suggested that I mention this since it would give the readers a better insight as to why I might have made the decisions I made in life. While they were not always the most level headed ones I admit, they were my survival mode ones that I felt worked at the time. Once more I thank you for your understanding.

I thank all of you for reading my book and I want to encourage anyone out there who has suffered from bi-polar or has gone through the horror of being molested to SEEK HELP. It is not YOUR FAULT. The only way that you will be able to deal with yourself without the guilt or the fear of it ever happening again is by getting help. I lived a long time using drugs to numb not only the pain from the injuries that I suffered from childhood, mental and physical, but just using them as some sort of crutch to further my need as another excuse to use for help. For example, if I used drugs then I would have an excuse to seek help with drugs rather than seek help with the REAL PROBLEM behind the drug use, which was the molestation. Once more, I thank you for reading my book and if it helps one person than it has helped me.

CHAPTER 1

My Formative Years

The main focus of my story is about my being an American woman who was held captive in an Iranian POW camp during the time of 9/11. It is also about the terrible tortures that I, and others, suffered at the hands of the guards while held captive. But it is important to understand my attitudes and the events which led up to my being in Iran.

I've always had a somewhat sarcastic sense of humor, but after being held captive for more than six weeks and tortured, I think these events brought out this characteristic in me even more. Thus, some people may be put off by my sense of sarcasm. However, if you had gone through all the things I did, whose to say how your own attitudes might be affected.

I was adopted into my family at the age of six months old.

I have two sisters and one brother in my adoptive family. My dad is as stubborn and chauvinistic as Archie Bunker. He always expected dinner on the table on time, and my mother's opinions were never given much merit. My mom, being the stay at home mother she was, had a sort of naiveness about her, but it was nothing that possibly a little education might have fixed. I think my father's attitudes had more to do with the generation he grew up in as well as my mother's. Both my parents are wonderful people and I couldn't possibly love or desire to have any other parents more than these two. As for my two sisters and brother, they are my parent's natural children.

The reason I was adopted was due to my biological parents abusing me, as well as my six other natural siblings. I was removed from their home and taken in as a foster child at first, then later adopted.

From what I've been told, all my natural siblings were adopted out separately. I learned later that my birth mother was mentally ill. I visited her in a mental institution once when I was fifteen. She would talk about the past and laugh as though it were a big joke. She had no sense of reality and what had happened to her children. I never had a desire to go see her again.

My biological father was apparently even worse. He would beat my mother senseless, and because of this, she was afraid to take the kids and leave. Keep in mind, this was in the mid 1960s when the laws were lax concerning spouse abuse.

Apparently my biological father had a fetish for dropping the kids on their heads on the cement for punishment. I'd heard that he served time in jail, but I don't think it had anything to do with the abuse. I know he suffered a bullet wound for running from the police.

I was kept in a closet for most of the six months I had lived with my biological parents. I had multiple cigarette burns on my arms and legs and had been fed only cow's milk for the first six months of my life, rather than baby formula. Therefore, I was malnourished. Also, I had never been given a bath in all that time.

Since I was adopted at six months old, I have no memory of my birth parents. So my adoptive parents are the only ones I consider my real parents. My mom is a hard worker who always took care of others.

For as long as I can remember, Mom had an Adult Foster Care Home where she took in the elderly and cared for them in our home. I used to sit and listen to these elderly patients and their stories.

I loved these people and defended them vigorously from my classmates at school who used to make fun of them, especially when the weather was nice. When I was dropped off at home after school and exited the bus, all these elderly people would be sitting out on our lawn in chairs, or walking around, and the kids in the bus would yell out, "Stop one, Night of the Living Dead!"

The Cat Farm

I used to collect cats, sort of, like people collect figurines. I bring this up here because my love for animals, and cats in particular, will come out later in my story. The only problem was, the cats ate food which cost my parents money. I also liked to read a lot. So my dad put a recliner out in the garage, so I could read and be with my cats.

Most of the cats were males. I would put butter on the paws of any cats in the neighborhood that frequented our yard. Scotty, my best friend and neighbor, who was also adopted, told me this would work to keep the cats hanging around my house. That way I could claim them as my own. One day when I came home from school, my mom met me at the bus.

She said, "Lori, your dad says you can't keep all these cats."

"Why not?" I cried. "They don't hurt anyone and they keep the mice population down, and they are my friends."

"Well, that's fine," my mother replied, "But there are no mice within a twenty mile radius of here due to your cats now, and one of your Morris's turned out to be a Maureen and had babies in the garage."

I went to see the kittens and they were so adorable I couldn't perceive of ever getting rid of any of them. My mom explained that the males would kill the kittens as part of their natural animal tendency. I couldn't believe the nerve of her telling me this about my loyal friends. Well, guess what happened? It ruined my ideology of animals ever being loyal to one another. Much to my dad's happiness, I allowed him to clean out the cats.

Being Spoiled

Now my adoptive parents are wonderful people. Sure, they have their flaws, as do any parents, but none I can hold against them to this day. They did, after all, have to deal with me and my siblings. Despite growing up with two very loving, kind, generous parents, I still had a wild streak in me that desired independence at an early age. By the time my parents adopted me, they were much more better off financially than when my brother and two sisters were younger. They tended to give me extravagant gifts, like the Christmas of 1979, which brings to mind another reason why my siblings probably despised me. I think my mom and dad felt they had to make up for the terrible abuse I'd suffered for the first six months of my life.

Scotty, my neighbor, and still best friend, received a new Sno-Jet snowmobile. I was jealous and knew one of the weaknesses my parents suffered was keeping up with the Joneses. I nonchalantly asked my dad if I could have a snowmobile for Christmas.

"What?" he asked. "I thought you wanted a new ten speed bike?"

"I did," I answered, "but since Scotty has this new Sno-Jet, I want to be able to go on snowmobile runs with him," I whined. My dad dismissed the idea ever-so-casually. I was sure I would never get one. But it was always nice to put the hint out there.

Christmas arrived, and I was getting nervous since there were only thirteen presents under the tree and none were the size of a ten-speed, let alone a snowmobile, although, there was this one strangely wrapped container that jingled on top. After unwrapping all the gifts that night – it was our tradition to unwrap gifts on Christmas Eve after the kids had outgrown Santa – the last gift I unwrapped was a gas can, with keys taped to the top. My dad was grinning like the Cheshire Cat. Yes, I had in fact received my snowmobile, a Ski-Doo 340, brand new, with an outfit to match. Did I scream in excitement? Did I dance around the house? No. I cried because I hadn't received my ten-speed bike, which, by-the-way, my mom was carrying up from the basement. A brand new Fuji 13-speed, I believe, but can't remember for sure. Score! Now I was content.

I had just turned thirteen years old. You can see by now how I was somewhat spoiled and headstrong even by that age. Are you starting to see the reasoning behind my siblings love/hate relationship with me?

By this age I was starting to get, what some people might call, a wild hair up my ass. I was restless. My body was starting to develop and I wanted something more than just the same old things, like school, homework, and playing with my best friend after school everyday. I can't really say what motivated me to evolve into this wild youth. I had absolutely no plans for what I wanted to do with my life or why I did the things I was doing. Still, to this day, I don't know why. Nonetheless, I caused my parents a lot of grief and heartache. And this they never deserved. Thank God they've lived long enough to see that none of it was their fault, nor was I bound to be like that forever. At least I hope I'm not.

I am just so thankful that when they chose to adopt me, they kept their promise to love me unconditionally. Some might say they did wrong by standing by me, regardless of how much pain I put them through, but I would disagree. When you choose to raise children, the most important factor, at least in my eyes, is for the parents to love their child unconditionally.

Yes, discipline is good, but ignoring a child, or withholding your love, or even allowing the child to believe you are withholding your love, is by far the worst crime in my eyes. Why? Because we already live in a world which is far too judgmental and critical of others as it is. Some people feel they have to compete for everything and if they aren't numero uno in their endeavors, they lose hope and the motivation of ever achieving anything more in life.

Women especially have it tough dealing with all kinds of self-esteem problems and when a person is given the gift of two parents who love them, no matter what, then they never lose hope or sight of their achievements. If I hadn't had my parents to come crying home to after some of my escapades, I don't even know if I'd be here right now.

To prove my point, I dropped out of school in the eighth grade, yet later went on to graduate in the top of my baccalaureate class (BSN) from college.

On To Independence

At the tender age of fifteen, I'd decided I needed to be on my own, so I got married. What kind of family allows this to happen to a young girl, you ask? One who has a daughter who threatens pregnancy if they don't sign the declaration of emancipation so I could go to Missouri and marry a much older guy.

I told you I had made many mistakes in my past and this was one of them. Would I have done it any differently, looking back? Probably not.

I had taken on the bad habit of lying to my parents as to my whereabouts when I went out with my friends. This started at the age of fourteen, and about this time, a hot new disco had opened up in a nearby town. I would tell my dad I was going roller-skating and that I'd be home no later than 1:00 a.m. The roller-skating rink was about twice as far as the disco, thus giving me more partying time.

The girl who drove was my friend's sister, and my dad believed the three of us were all going roller-skating every Friday and Saturday night. I'm sure my dad thought there were worse things we could be up to than roller-skating.

COULD and WERE! Every weekend after downing a few beers in the car, we went in to the disco and had our fun. While there, I ran into the guy who later became my first husband. Mike was most parents' dream date, though just not my parents' dream, due to his age. He was about six years older than me. In all fairness and honesty, Mike thought me to be closer to legal age – well, more like seventeen, almost eighteen.

Dad became somewhat suspicious of my weekly roller-skating events and decided to follow us one night. While I was in the disco and ready to head out to the car with my friends for another beer, my other friend, Jean, exclaimed as she ran back in, "Lori your dad's here!"

I ran into the bathroom, hoping that if he didn't see me all would be well. My dad has one good trait which was used that night, persistence. Actually two traits. He has no qualms about humiliating his kids if they disobey his wishes. He not only came into the disco, and yelled, stopping the music, but continued to go into the girl's bathroom (geesh), and dragged me out, past my friends, and out to the car.

All the while we drove home, I expected some harsh punishment. I only received one of those, "Where did your mother and I go wrong?" speeches. You know, those lectures you end up giving your own kids when you're older, but despise them at the age of fourteen.

Mike, who was at the disco when this happened, followed us home as well. I think I was more frightened to see his nice SUV following us (which in no way related to why I liked him), rather than my consequences upon arriving home. Once at home, Mike pulled in behind us. Mike asked my dad if he could come in and speak with him and my mother.

My dad, at this point, was speechless, and made some grunt and hand gesture which indicated "right this way."

Much to my surprise, Mike was very well-versed in parent speak, and told my parents of his undying love for me. When he found out my real age, this fact didn't seem to hinder him at all. My parents agreed he was a boy with a head on his shoulders, who worked a decent job and paid his bills; so, they agreed to let us keep dating.

The marriage thing eventually came up when I said I'd had enough of school and wanted to drop out and get married. Of course my parents protested.

We had a summer of confrontations with me leaving letters all over the house to ensure my mother would read them. They were letters to Mike, telling him that if my parents didn't let me get married, I would get pregnant, then we could legally go to Maryland and get married. This was the decisive factor in my parents allowing me to get married. I'm sure their decision had something to do with my threats to get pregnant if they didn't sign the paper work for emancipation.

By the way, Mike never knew about those letters. Had he, he would have lost respect for me, since he was such a decent guy. We were married in the summer of 1981, in Missouri, under the St. Louis Arch by some judge I connived into meeting us there. I was outfitted in my bridal apparel of halter-top and shorts, while Mike wore jeans and cowboy boots.

There you have the misguided judgments of a determined teenager. I actually knew what I was doing was wrong, but had made up my mind to get out of the house and have my own way. Now that I'm older, I see how disillusioned I was.

On To Strike Two

For reasons in order not to implement mudslinging, I will just say that Mike and I did not stay married very long. He confessed to marrying me because of my appearance, and the fact I had won every dance contest at our school. Which, by the way, was due to my brother taking me out hunting with him, then pointing his .22 rifle at my feet and telling me to dance. I guess I was trained to dance quite enthusiastically. Moreover, I only wed Mike to get out of the house and to achieve my independence.

Mike and I lasted approximately eight months, twenty-one days and four hours. Then we called it quits. Let's just say that I became bored with the life of being a teenaged housewife.

What was I to do now at the ripe old age of sixteen? I had quit school after the eighth grade, didn't have a High School diploma or a GED and was chomping at the bit to see the world. What could I do? At least I waited until my seventeenth birthday before I went on to my next mistake.

Be All That I Could Be – Mostly AWOL

At seventeen I joined the Army. I loved the ads since they gave me motivation for wanting to do something honorable, plus the fact I didn't really have any plans for the moment. You could say I was a bit impulsive, since I never even told my parents I'd joined until after I'd signed the papers and had a ship-out date. Because I had papers of emancipation, I didn't need my parent's permission to join.

Okay, hold on for error number two. I fell in love with my recruiter, who reciprocated, against all military rules and taboos. Therefore, when my ship-out date arrived, I had to enter the delayed enlistment program – due to my being pregnant. My beloved recruiter was stationed at Ft. Carson, Colorado at the time I found out about the pregnancy. He went AWOL and lost his military years for me. I in no way asked him to go AWOL. He called me one day and said, "I can't wait to see you."

I said, "Me, too." Five minutes later he was at my door. We planned to get married right away, but I wanted a traditional white gown wedding since I hadn't had one the first time around, and didn't want to be pregnant for it. So we waited until after the birth.

I had Douglas Edwin Bregg II, on December 23, 1983. I never knew the true meaning of love until I had him. I normally couldn't stand babies, until he came along. After Dougie was born there was nothing ugly about any of his actions, including that new born cry which used to irritate me with other babies.

He was the apple of my eye, and I did everything right for him, or so I had hoped. I couldn't stand to be away from him for fear I would miss one step, one smile, or one giggle that should be caught on camera.

My phone bill went sky high since I was living in Colorado at the time Doug was born at Pikes Peak Hospital in Colorado Springs. The husband, whom I hadn't married yet, was trying to save his military career, and my ship-out date wasn't until August of 1984.

We returned home to Michigan in February of '84. Doug finally got his less than honorable discharge from the military; and blames me to this day, I'm sure, for ruining his career. What did I do? I fell in love. Yes, but never once did I tell him to go AWOL. That was his own choosing – again and again and again.

In July of 1984, I considered myself physically pleasant enough to walk down the isle of matrimony in my new mother-in-law's yard to wed her son.

By August we were already fighting about my plans to stick it out with the military, and I thought we had agreed on things.

On the morning of MEPS (Military Enlistment Processing Station) ship-out, I asked him to take me to Detroit. He put the pillow over his head and wouldn't even kiss me good-bye.

I sat at the MEPS station awaiting my flight to Ft. Jackson, South Carolina, and watched Sgt. York on the TV. This is definitely not a show to watch on your ship-out date. It gives you way too many ideas on backing out prior to leaving. Conscientious objector, came to mind. I thought, maybe I should go up and talk to the Colonel and tell him I had suddenly changed my views. I did just that. It didn't work. He said there was no war going on then, but he couldn't blame me for trying.

I arrived in Ft. Jackson, scared shitless. Among the chaos was the shouting of drill sergeants who urged us, and taunted us, to find out what kind of recruits we were.

Then the big blow came. We were the new test recruits for an experimental training program. Rather than the usual eight week basic training that everyone else went through, we were chosen to go through a test cycle of thirteen weeks to find out if women could qualify for Combat MOS's. Military Occupational Specialty. Lucky me, I thought, now depressed.

We got settled in and the first day was just your general get-your-bunk-together and meet-the-sadistic-men-and-women-who-would-be-training-you and watching-you-forthe-next-thirteen-weeks – day.

I made some allies the first day, but also met the meanest girl in our barracks that day, too. Anna Aponte, a Mexican girl who grew up in the Bronx. We did not exactly hit it off, to say the least. Besides the drill Sergeants to worry about, I also had her breathing down my neck over some smartass comment I'd made in regards to her ruthless remark about this "dickhead place" we were in. I didn't know it yet, but she and I would soon become best friends. For the time being, though, I had to put up with her.

I went through the rigors of PT, Pugil Stick training, and hand-to-hand combat, and made it fine. As a matter of fact, I thought basic training was the best part of my short military career. Not to mention the only part I truly completed.

After six weeks we were finally allowed to call home. Joy, joy! I waited quite awhile in line to call my husband, with my eager heart pounding – only to hear my mother-in-law say in a shaky voice, "Doug moved to St. John's with some girl and took little Dougie with him."

That sure cheered me up, after waiting six weeks to hear this. So I went to my commander and told him I needed an emergency leave, and why.

The next thing I knew, my drill sergeant had me in his office, telling me not to let the bastard win . . . and to continue on with my training, and beat him at his own game. Not to mention, my sergeant was putting moves on this vulnerable girl.

I stayed in the military and was sleeping with my sergeant within twenty-four hours. The only problem was, we were caught, and he was put out of the camp, pending a military investigation. I graduated basic training, went home for my short leave between basic and AIT (Advanced Infantry Training), and thought Doug and I had worked out our problems, or his anyway.

I then arrived at Ft. Gordon, Georgia for AIT. What a blast. And I mean this literally. While there, I hooked up with a girl named Missy. She and I became all too well known at the base. I met Missy during the first two weeks and we hit it off. We had a similar sense of humor, and our attitudes on life in the military were the same.

Missy and I both had our share of problems with authority, and also had much more in common, like both not giving a shit about being put on extra duty when we disrespected the officers. And we were both on the short side. I say this last since it had a lot to do with how we were treated when our platoon had to march, or do PT in cadence.

Since Missy and I were the shortest ones in the platoon, or

battalion for that matter, they let us lead the formation for marches or PT. Their second reason for doing this was when they let us "fall in" freely, Missy and I always chose the back, so we could gab, and try to lose the formation if we became tired, which meant eventually ending up at the PX shopping, then returning to be counseled by our Platoon Sergeant.

Therefore, the whole base eventually knew us, at first for our supposed "cuteness," then because our first AWOL stint became the laugh of the century.

One day Missy and I had literally become so fed up with the military that we decided we needed a break, or at least some time for ourselves. We promptly went AWOL right after receiving our pay checks.

We went to Atlanta, got a room at the Ramada Inn, and had planned to stay the weekend, then turn ourselves in. We needed a weekend of partying together and a chance for us just to be girls, instead of soldiers.

We went shopping and bought some beautiful dresses for a party we heard the Ramada Inn was having that night. We returned to our rooms, went to the pool, and enjoyed all the benefits of the hotel, while getting severely drunk off our asses. Then came the time for the party. We got dolled up and planned to make a grand entrance, at least that's how we pictured it in our minds.

Our hotel room was on the top floor, therefore we took the stairs down so we could enter the ballroom via a set of country-style winding stairs where we could view the guests from above. We were drunk, and didn't notice all the uniforms at first as we came strolling down the stairs like two Scarlet O'Haras.

The first person we ran into was our Captain – who, by the way, knew we were AWOL. He immediately had the MPs take us back to the base and put us under house arrest. So much for our grand entrance. It was a military ball, and no one had told us.

AWOL Again

After about two weeks, once I had gotten off the LOP (Loss of Privileges) for going AWOL the first time, I finally decided I'd had enough of military life and wanted to leave without Missy this time. Also, there were several officers and higher enlisted men, whom my First Sergeant insisted I testify against who were also at the ball. I, on the other hand, saw no reason for ruining a perfectly good pension for someone based on the events of a one night fling (also known as fraternization). I guess, since I was supposed to testify against several men, this might be considered several flings.

Yes, I became wild. I'm not sure if it was due to being away from home and responsibility, or because I wanted to get even with my husband, who was still cheating on me back home. Or it could of been that I just enjoyed it. But if you tell this to anyone, the term "double standards" often applies. Meaning, if you are a man, you're considered a stud, but a woman is considered a whore.

After a week of being AWOL, and living off vending machine food, and Dexatrim, I called Missy. I was deathly ill, running a fever, throwing up, and generally weak. Probably from the Dexatrim and vending food. Missy immediately became worried and called the MPs to pick me up. She came with them.

When I looked out the motel window and saw an MP car, with one MP and Missy with him, I thought it was a joke. But then she said, "I didn't want you to die in the outbacks of Georgia." I was admitted to the hospital with two MPs stationed outside my door.

I was resting in bed when the nurse came in to tell me my brother was on the phone. My brother? He hadn't talked to me in years. Well, it wasn't.

The caller turned out to be one of the men I was supposed to testify against after I was discharged – from the hospital, that is.

He had the perfect plan. He would call when the MPs took their meal break at midnight, which only left a nurse to be distracted by his phone call, thus allowing me to sneak out of the room and down the stairs to the service elevator. This was where he would be waiting to take me to the Greyhound Bus Station for a ride home, to Michigan.

Brilliant, I thought. What a guy! At midnight, sure enough, the guards went on break, thinking me to be fast asleep. And, sure enough, the phone rang. The only problem I had was not knowing about applying pressure when you take out an IV. I had blood everywhere while trying to get my civilian clothes out of the locker and get the hell out of the room in this short time.

Minutes later, I was running down the stairs, while at the same time changing into my clothes out of the hospital attire. Blood was everywhere. Then, I ran into some people coming up the stairs. It must have looked like I was escaping a heinous crime scene.

I did manage to get out and was taken by my pal over the border of Georgia into South Carolina, to catch the Greyhound for home. This escape went well, except – and I should have expected no less than this – I think what came next should have been a wake-up call of what could have happened, but didn't. My military career was spinning out of control, along with my sanity, as well as my complete disregard for authority.

I know I was taking wild risks, I was doing things I shouldn't have. Things seemed to happen to me, what can I say – they just do.

When the bus pulled out of the station, my every intention was for a straight shot to Detroit. Wrong. The bus had to make a stop first. Where, you ask?

When I saw the sign that said, "Welcome to Ft. Gordon," I immediately became ill and ran to the back of the bus, flattening myself on the floor under the last seat, and kept my legs tucked close to my body. I felt sure it was a set up. But it wasn't. They always made this stop to pick up the military personnel who were going on leave. But trust me, I would have never even boarded the bus had I known about the stop.

I didn't feel comfortable again until I saw the sign, "You Are Now Leaving Ft. Gordon."

Staying Mobile

I arrived back home, tried to patch things up with my husband, and decided to go to truck driving school to stay mobile and out of the hands of the MPs who were trying to catch me for being AWOL. Also for the little problem of wanting me to testify against those poor guys who had their careers and pensions to lose.

I loved truck driving. It was a freedom I had never experienced before – and I could take my son Dougie with me. Too much fun! He was between two and four years old during this time.

I even bought him his own cowboy hat and boots for the road trips. He talked on the CB quite regularly. The truckers adored Dougie, and loved his talks at night to keep them alert. Dougie, in turn, felt like quite the big shot on the CB, until I started to notice his vocabulary changing – and not for the better. He was grounded off the CB for a while. My husband drove truck too, so we never saw much of each other. As it turned out, one of the women he was cheating on me with, was my sister. Now you can see why I had a kind of love/hate relationship with some of my siblings. She had done this to me before with one of my boyfriends.

I drove truck for most of the next couple of years.

After I left Ft. Gordon I was finally caught about two years later. Eventually the MPs caught up with me and I was flown to Kentucky for out-processing. I resisted testifying, thus saving a few guys their asses, as well as their pensions. I eventually received my discharge papers.

Finally out of my military career, I started going to college in my spare time. I changed majors almost as much as I did my underwear, and eventually got divorced from husband number two on the basis of Domestic Violence and Adultery. This was in 1987. We'd been married a little over three years. Again, to avoid mudslinging, I will not delve into this part of things.

Now on to the next chapter of my life, and my plunge into hell.

CHAPTER 2

My Next Husband

I met my next husband, Mohammad Foroozandeh, in August of 1993, while I was attending Northern Michigan University. I was twenty-seven years old and went to school full time while I worked part time as a waitress. My son Dougie was nine years old. Mohammad was in the Upper Peninsula of Michigan, which is across the Mackinaw Bridge, visiting his children from a previous marriage, to an Elizabeth Stewart, who was also attending college for her CPA degree. Her two children's names were Farid (Sean), and Farah (Shannon) Stewart. His ex-wife, Elizabeth, had tried to warn me as to why she had moved up to Marquette. With the help of authorities, she had undergone a complete name change, from her married name and maiden name. She told me Mohammad had been violent and took her to Iran as well. She was a very intelligent woman, who could speak and write in Farsi, and knew a lot about their culture.

One night, when we both discovered how Mohammad had been playing us, she came over (she lived next door in the University Campus Housing) and we got drunk and talked. She told me how violent he was and how much he adored Iran, but preferred living in the United States for undisclosed reasons, and that in order to get her children and herself away from Mohammad, she had changed her name and moved to a different town where no one knew her.

The only problem was Mohammad had managed to still capture her heart as well as change her mind and she ended up telling him where she was located.

Why didn't I listen? Because the reasons she gave were due to him being an undercover informant for KVET, an acronym for "Kalamazoo Valley Enforcement Team" who are DEA agents for Kalamazoo County, in Michigan. His partner was a guy named Tim, and she told me that Tim had screwed too many drug addicts by

15

buying drugs from them, then turning them in. At the same time, he also manipulated the authorities by bribing the addicts, and during many raids, he would only turn in about half of what he confiscated. So Elizabeth was getting death threats because of his partner's dealings. This is why she took her kids and relocated. I might add that she said Mohammad had a bad addiction to drugs as well. This didn't deter me as I had some issues of my own at the time.

Did I listen? Nooo! That seems to be a part of my personality, I just don't listen to other people's advice.

I thought she was a jealous woman who was trying to dissuade me from what I deemed to be a very attractive and powerful man.

Mohammad and I eventually moved in together. We lived together for about two and a half years before we got married in a Muslim wedding and relocated to Saginaw, Michigan, upon my graduation from nursing school. Once in Saginaw, Mohammad met with his brother, Abbas. The family had bought Abbas' way out of Iran, rather than let him stay to serve his two years in the military there. I need to add here that Mohammad served his two years during the Iran/Iraq war and was stationed on the border of Turkey, and has many scars from bullet wounds he received while in battle. Also, I'd like to add that all the time during our dating he advocated his support for the Shah, and was one of those students much into politics in 1979. He came to the USA to attend Western Michigan University where he obtained his Bachelors Degree in Automotive Engineering.

I believe he started out working for Chrysler to build a template for some new model of automobile. Also in his past was a job at James River in Kalamazoo which ended in a big lawsuit where he collected quite a bit of money. However, while he was with me I never saw any of it. He said it was already spent, but how, I'm not sure. He may have invested the money into the two car dealerships he owned.

He supposedly caught his arm in a big roller which was used to flatten large sheets of paper or cardboard. It caught accidentally on a glove he was wearing. The machine pulled his right arm in and fed it into the two rollers up to his shoulder. Because of this, they had to insert metal rods into his arm and reattach it. This is why airport security was very lax with him, due to the internal metal. Of course this was long before the time of 9/11 when airport security wasn't as tight as it is now.

We never owned a house, but rented a large house on Lake Superior and later a nice condo in Saginaw and lived quite well. I never had to help pay bills and any money I earned from my nursing was mine to keep and do whatever I wanted with it. His brother Abbas also lived with us. They worked together at the car dealerships. Abbas had more than enough money to get his own place, but never did. Mohammad always told me that it was customary in his culture for families to live together.

In Saginaw things were going along fine and Mohammad was running his two auto dealerships, and coaching soccer for appearance's sake, with my son from my other marriage who by now was about twelve. Mohammad did everything right for a while. If my son wanted a birthday party, Mohammad would go overboard to show his wealth, and rent a roller rink if that was Doug's wish. I thought it was due to his love for me and my son, but boy, I was sadly mistaken.

I later on realized he was collecting some kind of donations, for whatever cause he was collecting for, from the more elite people in the neighborhood, so appearances were really important to Mohammad.

* * *

Appearances counted in some areas, anyway. Mohammad was addicted to crack cocaine and heroine, but I didn't know it at the time, since he was supposed to be working undercover as a narc, which put him in contact with the drugs and the dealers. This was on top of his regular work at the car dealerships.

He sometimes took me down to the slum side of Saginaw and showed me the houses where he'd buy the drugs from, then raid them. He told me they used marked bills to purchase the drugs, then after the deal and arrests were made, the lead officer would pat Mohammad down to ensure he didn't get any extra drugs on the side. Soon this became an all too familiar routine, and the officers eventually quit patting him down. Thus it opened a wide door for corruption by Mohammad.

He sometimes disappeared for days at a time, and I was naive enough to think he was on legitimate drug buying sprees for the cops. Once I pulled in behind his car on one of the slum streets he'd showed me, and I took the chance of going up to the door of the house.

Mohammad answered the door and was high as a kite, and highly paranoid.

He accused me of bringing down the cops to catch him, along with every other thing he could accuse me of.

After that incident, we took a while to determine if our marriage was going to work out. We eventually decided to stay together and vowed to work through this. However, only a couple of weeks after these promises were made, he took me on another trip to the slum side of Saginaw. Mohammad said he just wanted me to meet some of the boys he dealt with. Why this was important to him, I had no clue. But later I found out he was trying to buy dope and exchange money for it in a quickie hand shake technique he was trying to perfect. The only problem was, it didn't work out that way.

Three black men were walking alongside the road when Mohammad pulled up to them and asked how they were doing. All of a sudden, one man reached in through the car window and grabbed Mohammad around the neck. The other two were trying to get into the back seat, but I pushed the power lock button down, and tried to roll up the windows via the power button on the side where Mohammad was being held around the neck. Apparently these people had found out he was a narc, a dirty one to boot, and weren't too happy about it.

So there you have it. The man I thought who loved me with all his heart, risked not only his own life, but that of his wife as well, just to buy a little dope.

Why did I stay with him? Because I loved him, and I was determined to make this marriage work after going through two previous failed ones. Besides, I was like most women who are oblivious to the fact you can't make a leopard change his spots.

* * *

After a while Mohammad started to disappear for days on end, and I thought it was due to his drug addiction, but now, after knowing him better and in hind-site, I realize it was probably something else. There were too many phone calls that were incoherent, like he was hiding something, which I could tell the difference, not to mention the extreme miles put on our car. But his brother Abbas, who lived with us and never used any illegal drugs, would always disappear at the same time Mohammad was gone. So, looking back, I believe there was something more going on than what I knew about. If it was just drugs, it would be more practical to just stay in one place and get high, like most addicts do. Driving over 1000 miles in one weekend didn't make any sense to me. I wonder now if he had made trips to Canada for some reason. I never did find out what he was up to. I was quite naive about most of his activities.

Mohammad was an excellent manipulator. People used to say he could talk you out of your raincoat in a hail storm. However, I was now a nurse with high aspirations and wanted to continue my education and have a successful career in research. I also had my own problems to deal with.

Not to make excuses for myself here, but I might as well tell the truth. I had become addicted to the prescription drug Vicodin and I was up to about sixty pills a day. I had several ways of either writing false prescriptions, or calling them in. All this had been going on long before I'd met Mohammad. It was the result of a car accident a few years before.

Here's what happened: I was coming home from the Casino in Sault Ste Marie, Michigan, and my truck went out of control on black ice. It rolled about four or five times. I had no seat belt on – this was before there were seat belt laws – and managed to crawl out after finding myself lying on the other side of the cab, under the dashboard. My boyfriend, who was following me home at the time, took me to the hospital. The boyfriend I mention here was before I met Mohammad. The reason I was driving so recklessly was because I'd just found out this boyfriend had lied to me and was actually married. So I'd left the Casino angry. My dad had just given me the Ford truck and I felt bad about rolling it. I think the only reason I wasn't killed is because I was slightly drunk and just rolled with the truck. Not to excuse drinking and driving here. I'm just glad no one else was involved in the accident.

I had no visible injuries, just a scraped knee, but I was in a lot of pain. My back and neck were killing me. The now ex-boyfriend, as of that night, took me to the hospital and dropped me off, then just left without telling me. The doctors gave me the Vicodin, as well as Demerol and Morphine for the severe back trauma, as well as muscle relaxers. I was in the hospital for two nights. When I was released they sent me home with more Vicodin. The neurologist and an orthopedic surgeon suggested taking the Vicodin long term. Then after one year, they abruptly stopped it. Cold turkey, no weaning me off it. However, my back still hurt quite often, so I found different ways to get the pain reliever. I wasn't looking to get high from it. But rather looking forward to a few hours of relief from the constant pain. Therefore, I was already addicted to the Vicodin when I met Mohammad.

By this time my liver had started to fail, so I was admitted to the Mayo Clinic where I underwent some testing and was told that my liver was in serious trouble.

Well, no shit, I thought. But being the true nursing professional I was, I could not tell them the <u>truth</u> as to <u>why</u> my liver was failing. In other words, I gave them a false medical history and let the so-called experts figure it out for themselves.

That was my justification as an addict. But, they couldn't figure it out. It was because of this I lost a lot of respect for the Mayo Clinic. Upon returning home to Michigan from Minnesota, where the Mayo Clinic is located, I finally came clean with my nursing supervisor and requested an inpatient rehab.

She sent me to HealthSource, a rehab center for professionals such as doctors and nurses. This rehab center, which resembled the one in the movie "The Dream Team," with Michael Keaton, was worse than any I'd heard about. But, I had to view it in some manner in order to get through it.

A lot had happened to me in my past and humor was always my escape, even if it was dry and sarcastic at best.

When I finally walked out of the rehab center, guess who had Vicodin waiting for me? And you don't know how much I craved it at this point. Going through Vicodin withdrawals was a hell of a lot worse than heroin, since for as long as I'd been taking it, it had absorbed into my bone tissue. And to be honest, when I got into that serious car accident in 1991, no one thought I'd live through it. So even after going through the withdrawals and becoming clean, I still had a lot of back pain to deal with. That never went away.

In all respect to Mohammad and my blaming him, he didn't have to do too much convincing. Therefore, I slid back into my previous habits. Life went on and I was eventually caught for prescription fraud.

Mohammad told me we could easily get away from all my shitty legal problems. He was once again working as an undercover narcotics agent on the side, for BAYNET, the DEA in Bay City and Saginaw. He somehow convinced the judge to release me on personal recognizance. Then Mohammad talked me into leaving the country with him. He promised that nothing would happen to me in Iran, and that I could still pursue my nursing, and work without any problems. Despite all my troubles with the Vicodin, I had managed to graduate in December of 1995 with a degree in nursing near the top of my class and I enjoyed my work.

And because I was his wife, this automatically made me an Iranian citizen. He explained that Iran was quite modern now, not like most people thought it to be. This made me feel a little better about going.

By this time Dougie was about fifteen years old and I gave him the choice of staying in the USA to live with his dad, or go with us to Iran. I didn't feel right about forcing him to go with us into a foreign country that I still knew nothing about. Besides, Dougie had always wanted to try living with his father. I figured at fifteen he was mature enough to make his own decision and it would be okay. So we made arrangements for Dougie to move in with his father.

Mohammad sold his car dealerships before we left. His brother stayed in the United States and tied up a lot of the loose ends for us, since we left in such a hurry. We had married in 1996 and left for Iran in May of 1998.

I eventually boarded a plane at JFK Airport, knowing that I had a warrant out for my arrest, but not really knowing what Mohammad's true intentions were, since it had all happened so fast. As I said, he was a master manipulator.

I swallowed several Vicodin and boarded the plane. Next stop was the IRI, or Islamic Republic of Iran.

CHAPTER 3

Iran

The plane trip lasted about twenty-two hours, with a stop over at Heathrow Airport in London, England before coming to Mehrab International Airport in Tehran, Iran. While on the plane to Iran, Mohammad began to change with each mile we successfully traveled. It struck me as odd when we finally got over Islamic territory, that instead of nicely telling me to don my hejab, he barked it.

As we got close to the airport we circled a lake, I remember, about a zillion times, prior to landing, and I was becoming quite nervous. I never liked airplanes to begin with, and when we had boarded this one in London, it really didn't seem like the safest one to ride on. A DC-9 which had electrical malfunctions that kept making the lights flicker. Not to mention the big bang we heard upon takeoff. The Captain finally came on the intercom after we were completely airborne, about twenty minutes later, after all the passengers had already secured their standing near each exit. He said in a quite nervous tone, "We hope you're enjoying your flight en route to Tehran Mehrab Airport. The noise you heard at the beginning of the flight was nothing to concern yourself with, this was just the airplane letting off a little built up energy."

I had to laugh, because the last time I checked, airplanes did not need to release built up carbon, but hey, I was willing to believe anything to get through this. But I noticed my fearless hubby, upon hearing this, downed about four Vicodin and disappeared into the bathroom for about the next half hour, and left me with only five Vicodin and three Valium. So what a ride we had.

Upon arrival in Tehran, the first thing I felt uncomfortable with was how they immediately kept <u>my</u> passport, but not my husbands. I was an American and was supposed to be independent and keep my own belongings, but Mohammad said this was standard procedure and not to worry. He said we would apply to get it back after arriving in Shiraz. "Okee-dokee," I said. Little did I know then how much red tape I would go through later on when I tried to leave Iran. But more on that later.

The next incident concerned a bunch of videos I had brought with us which customs was not going to allow us to keep. Mohammad told me to flirt with the man to distract him so he could throw some of our suitcases over to the "already been inspected pile," verses the "awaiting to be inspected pile." So I did as he said. After all, my Farsi was minimal and I needed my American movies. It was quite odd that before we left home he deemed it necessary to buy three sets of American Touristor luggage that looked exactly alike. I guess this would be enough to screw up a busy guy inspecting luggage at the airport while flirting with an American woman.

After finally getting many of the videos and other non-admittable items released, we were picked up by a friend of Mohammad's in Tehran, in a very expensive car.

Tehran was much more modern than I'd imagined. The skyline resembled any big city in America. It was very smoggy, too, which is also similar to many big cities in America. Yes, Mohammad was right, the country had become more modern, in buildings and beauty anyway.

One thing that bothered me, while we were on our way to his friend's house, there was a parade, or march going on in the street. All these men were marching with bags attached to what looked like chains slung around their shoulders. They chanted something, then whipped the chains and allowed the bags to hit them as hard as they could on their backs. I asked Mohammad what this was all about. He told me it had something to do with paying tribute to Hossein, who was Ali's son, and Ali was the successor of Muhamad the Prophet in Shi'a Muslim beliefs.

The difference, I learned later, between the Sunni and the Shi'a was who had succeeded Muhamad the Prophet. The Sunnis were more Arab based people, and believed that the older, wiser Omar had succeeded Muhamad. While the Shi'as believe that the younger Ali succeeded him. This sect is less Arab based and more Persian based. And please, if you learn nothing else from this book, never confuse an Arab for a Persian. They are highly prejudiced of one another, and they both think their ethnic heritage is above the others.

Getting back to Tehran. One thing I noticed was there seemed to be only <u>one</u> kind of car that <u>everybody</u> owned. Mohammad told me the cars were called Peykans. They had been around since the 1950's or before, and were built in Iran. They weren't the prettiest of cars, but were sturdy.

Another thing that struck me as odd, was how the women walked behind the men when out in public. Mohammad had told me before we left America that they didn't practice this custom any longer in Iran – well apparently they still did. And if the woman got too close in proximity to the man, she was smacked in the face like a dog. I saw this take place while waiting at a stop light. Mohammad told me not to worry about it, those were fanatics who insisted on behaving that way, and Shiraz was totally different than Tehran. He had told me that most people in Tehran loved and worshiped the Ayatollah, thus breeding fanaticism . . . while the majority of people from Shiraz worshiped and missed the Shah.

The Shah was more pro-Western. He tried hard to make Iran a more Westernized society. The stories I'd heard regarding the changes that had been made while Reza Pahlivi, The Shah, was in control of the country, was that they had nightclubs to dance in, pool halls, and women didn't have to wear chadors or scarves. Chadors are the big black, one piece coverings you wrap around you from your head to your toe. These are too complicated for my taste since you have to hold them together after you figure out how to get them on. I admire those women, who can carry a baby in one arm and pull a grocery cart down the sidewalk with the other, all the while keeping her chador in place. This became my new found goal for the moment, how to don and wear a chadora . . . and most importantly, how to keep it on.

I had been wearing a <u>roose a rees</u> which means scarf or head covering in Farsi. These scarves covered your hair. Women were not to show any skin or hair in public, and should never look any man in the eyes except for her husband. Otherwise she might be accused of the intent to commit adultery. Or if the husband really wanted to end his relationship, he only needed to <u>accuse</u> the wife of adultery and have a witness, then the wife could be executed.

Execution . . . yes, this brings to mind another first I witnessed while in Tehran. There was a big square in the middle of town with a huge crane in the center. I thought it must be used for some kind of construction, until I glanced up and saw a person hanging at the end of the crane. I gasped in horror, but Mohammad told me not to feel sorry for him, he was only getting what he deserved. I asked how he knew this, since he didn't know what the man's crime was? Mohammad just rolled his eyes and said in a sarcastic tone, "If the USA had laws like Iran does, and punishment like Iran does, there would be a hell of a lot less crime." Then he continued his tirade, "The USA gives their criminals cable TV, basketball courts and three square meals a day." Then he concluded, "This is what contributes to the USA's high crime rate."

He had me convinced, but I still couldn't see hanging someone in that barbaric way. They would tie the man to the end of the crane and slowly lift it in order to allow the man to suffer for about twenty minutes before he finally died of suffocation or strangulation. The part that bothered me the most was that they allowed and <u>encouraged</u> children to watch these public executions.

Shiraz is a city not far from the Caspian Sea, and some of the most beautiful sites are in this town. In Tehran, however, I was not afforded that many sightseeing opportunities.

Another thing about Iran is there are no department or grocery stores. You buy your vegetables and fruits at a produce stand, your rice and sugar at another store, and your meat from yet another. So the women get used to hauling grocery carts up and down the streets on less than perfect sidewalks.

Tehran is much more crowded than Shiraz, and is about twelve hours by bus from Shiraz. But Tehran definitely has more to offer than Shiraz in categories like clothing, gifts to send to <u>Amrika</u> (which is how they pronounce America).

The one thing I spotted, and was very happy to see, was the open affection shared between people who are out in public. Persians always say hello if they see someone they know while out walking. Then they go through a ten minute ritual of kissing each member on both cheeks and looking like they're interested in whatever is said. This open affection is only between members of the same sex since men and women are not allowed to touch each other in public, unless they are married. The nice thing was they truly seemed to be interested in each other's lives. But later I was to learn why. This is the gossip capital of the world!

Getting back to our arrival in Tehran and Mohammad's friend. His friend, who lived in a very nice house, sure kept my husband busy the first week-end we were there. All this was quite strange, since Mohammad told me we'd be going straight to Shiraz. Well, I discovered that Mohammad was doing sniffable heroin with this friend. This was by accident. Well, sort of. I was a nosey (foozel) person, and did manage to find things out, if given enough time to look, which made Mohammad quite nervous about me. But I've always said, if you're honest, then you have nothing to hide or to worry about. I know what you're thinking. This coming from a person who left America because of a warrant for false prescriptions.

They had come back from a short trip on a Saturday, and Mohammad dropped off all his stuff in the bedroom, then went to take a shower, so I started going through his pants and found several wrapped papers of what looked like light brown powder. I didn't know the name of it at the time, since I only thought you could inject heroin. I didn't know you could sniff it.

When we went out that night on the streets of Tehran, I, being the confrontist I am, asked him about it. As a result I became engaged in a marathon. Good thing I wasn't wearing sandals, or I may not have gotten far enough away to scream, "I didn't touch it, you bastard."

That settled him down, until he realized that his American wife had just called him a "bastard" in public on the streets of Tehran. This motivated him into yet another frenzy, where I once again got far enough away to scream, "Look, nobody here can probably understand English," then added, "But they will understand this. Pedar Sagh." I got into a taxi and was in the lead by a Peykan or two (taxis in Iran), but out of luck without any rials or tomans to pay the driver with. When we arrived at the door of his friend's house, which I knew Mohammad would not display his anger, I kindly told the taxi driver that my husband, who had just pulled up, would pay the fare.

As you can see, things started off sort of rocky upon my arrival in Iran. We stayed in Tehran about four days before heading off to Shiraz where Mohammad's family lived.

CHAPTER 4

Arriving in Shiraz

The flight from Tehran to Shiraz was only about two hours. However if you travel by bus, it is a dusty twelve hour trip. Once we finally managed to get to Shiraz, the Foroozandeh family greeted us. To me this was quite overwhelming. They had brought flowers and a wrapped package, which I was dying to open. But to my surprise, upon opening it was this thing that resembled a big black tent. I wondered if we were going to have to sleep outside until we found independent housing. All too soon I realized that neither was to be true. That is, we would not sleep outside, nor would we ever be required to have independent housing. The package contained a <u>chador</u> for me to wear while in public. His family wanted me into the Muslim attire as soon as possible. While I was being greeted by Mohammad's family I could swear I was receiving the so-called "evil eye," while my husband received praise and adoration. At the same time, he was being asked, "Why another American wife?" and "Why doesn't she know Farsi?"

We were whisked away almost as soon as we got off the plane in Shiraz. Once in the car at the airport, my husband kindly instructed me as to how to wear the big black tent. Then, without any options in his voice, he said to put it on NOW!

We arrived at what would soon become known as home sweet home. There was a large crowd awaiting us, complete with one slaughtered lamb for me, the proverbial animal lover, to step over. I did as tradition expected, and smiled while doing so. The house we would be living in was located on Afifabad Street. This street was in a very upper class neighborhood of Shiraz. I think Shiraz is the second largest city in Iran with the capital city of Tehran being the largest.

Again, the first thing I noticed was that all the cars were the same no matter where we drove. There was your occasional imported Ford

Fiesta or a Honda, but mostly people drove the Peykans, which are the Iranian built cars. To me they were ugly, hideous. Nothing nice about them. Thank God my husband had the decency to have foreign cars available for us. But remember, this is from the viewpoint of an American girl who grew up in the land of opportunity where everyone strives to be different in some way. And owning as well as seeing many kinds of cars is part of that diversity. We have choices in America.

When we arrived at the alley (I wouldn't call it a driveway) where our house/apartment was located, there was an odd smell that I couldn't quite determine. Sort of a cross between a dead body and a sewer.

I learned later that the pest control people had been there earlier to extinguish the cockroaches. "Cockroaches?" I asked in an uptight voice to Mohammad. "Why are there cockroaches?" His reply was that everyone had them, so I'd better learn to deal with them. Boy, he wasn't kidding, either!

When I first walked through a large steel, prison-type door, which was the entrance for the two apartments upstairs, I could see hundreds of dead roaches scattered on the stairs and floor. It looked like the Iwo Jima of roachville and I was horrified that this many cockroaches were co-existing with humans.

We had to go up three flights of stairs to reach our apartment. I heard laughter and voices before I walked into a room crammed full of people. They started grabbing me and kissing me on each cheek and saying, "This is Lori jan?" Jan is pronounced like June and means "dear one."

I had no idea who these people were, but was relieved they had been so enthusiastic to greet me. Mohammad was also grabbed and kissed by various relatives, and by the end of the night, I had gotten a little tired of being kissed and just wanted to sleep. I'm sure I appeared a little standoffish to some. I was accused of this by various relatives, mostly the women, like great aunts, or cousins, who'd had their eyes on Mohammad for their own daughters. I'm sure they resented him for bringing back another American wife when there were so many Iranian women for him to choose from. Remember, in Iran, the marriages are normally arranged between the man and the woman's parents. If a girl likes a man, she relays this to her parents who will meet with the man's parents, and then reach a conclusion as to whether he is good enough, or at least someone they desire their daughter to marry. This is usually the case, if you have fair minded parents who respect your wishes at all. However, some parents just pick out a rich, much older man to hook their daughters to. This is to ensure wealth in the family. But most parents are fair and respectful of their child's wishes.

The house consisted of two bedrooms, and two bathrooms, one of them an American bathroom with a real toilet seat you can actually sit down on. The other was your typical Iranian bathroom which consisted of a ceramic encased hole in the floor for you to squat over. Needless to say, not many people do much reading in the bathrooms of Iran. There was a small kitchen and a nice-sized living room and dining room. The apartment was cute and had balconies off both bedrooms that faced the street below which was tree lined. The house could have definitely used an interior decorator's touch, but was far from a hovel.

The first night at "modar bozorg's house," (mother-in-law's), was quite the night to remember. And full of tears. Everyone welcomed Mohammad home. We first sat and talked with the very large family, or I should say, my husband talked while I sat feeling stupid. However, once dinner was under way, I thought it would take some of the stress off. Boy was I wrong. Dinner was full of "pass this," and "Pass that," and something I became all too familiar with named "Toruf," which was the Persian's way of being overly polite while trying to make you obese at the same time. You could finish an eight course meal and they would still be offering you more, and insisting you eat it.

I did this for about the first two months, then I finally took a bold stand and at every meal would offer the prayer, then add, "Allah wishes no other human being here with us now, nor those who happen by, after once beginning our meal, to offer Lori any more food than what she bestows on her plate, Amen." This was usually good for a laugh, but it got the point across. Therefore, my waistline and pant size were saved for a while anyway.

After dinner that first night, Mohammad made us a bed in the back room, which was originally part of the dinning room, but had been sectioned off so there were more rooms. His sister, Nikoo, and her husband, Hamid, were still living there with their one year old son, Sena. They had been taking care of Mohammad's mother who was paralyzed on one side due to a stroke she'd suffered a couple of years back. Despite her stroke, she was very independent and got around well. Being a nurse, I was expected to take over the care of my new mother-in-law. Until his sister's family moved out of the second bedroom, we were given the back space.

I remember lying there and staring at the ceiling, wondering if I was going to fit in with the Iranian culture, but more importantly, would I be accepted by Mohammad's relatives. Being accepted into a family is very important in Iran and can make or break you, literally. They can give you a lot of grief for marrying someone they don't approve of. My mental attitude was that I was willing to adjust to anything as long as I was with my husband. I loved Mohammad deeply, and he had been there for me when I was most vulnerable. After all, he took me away from the USA and all my legal problems, I thought. Therefore I was willing to do whatever it took to fit in.

We were discussing how to fix up the apartment when all of a sudden Mohammad told me to hold still and not move. He then flicked a huge cockroach off my head that was trying to nest in my hair. I almost threw up. I screamed and told him to forget fixing up the house, let's get rid of those damned roaches first and foremost. He told me it was impossible, they were everywhere, since the sewer system ran underground – funny, I thought all sewers did this – and they had these literal highways underground and were in everyone's houses because they used the toilets as their exits and entrances. This was probably because most Iranian toilets were just a hole in the floor that you squat over, whereas American toilets have a water trap that prevents bugs from getting in, at least this way. I realize there are other ways for roaches to get into a house. However, just the thoughts of this really freaked me out, since all I could imagine was sitting on the toilet one day and have a cockroach emerge from between my legs. I'm sure I would pass out and hit my head on the bathtub (the bathroom was small) and die due to the cockroach. When I told Mohammad of this we laughed until we cried, then fell asleep in each other's arms.

The first week or two went by rather quickly with all the people coming to wish us well and to bring gifts of food, plants, or other small items. Nikoo, his sister, asked me if I wanted to go out shopping for a <u>montou</u>, and I agreed, though Mohammad came with us. It seemed like he never wanted to leave me alone and I was soaking up all his attention. When we got home that night I recalled in my mind the events of my first shopping trip in Iran.

I had seen so many different types of raincoats and none of them looked flattering to wear, but I supposed this was the point. The scarves a woman could choose from, though, were beautiful. They had scarves of every color and fabric imaginable. They had some very nice clothing boutiques in Iran. I found out that hardly any women wear dresses unless it was for a formal occasion, like a wedding. Also, to wear jeans meant you had a position within the financial world of Iran, meaning you obviously had money. I hadn't considered this anything special since jeans are so common in the USA. I really didn't understand how much this meant until I started to notice how much you were respected within the framework of society according to your wealth.

My husband had told me when we first met that he was related to the Shah, Reza Pahlavi, who was the Shah and leader of Iran during the revolution of 1979. I also learned about Mohammad's part during the Iran/Iraq war. He had been a soldier stationed on the northern border of Turkey and Iran. I guess this is where he and his battalion had endured a long conflict with Iraqi soldiers and this is where he was shot in the leg. He still had the nasty scar, but I never asked him about it. I figured he would tell me when he wanted to, and he eventually did. But the reason I mention his relationship to the Shah was because we lived on the same road as the Shah. Reza lived with his wife Farah, whom my husband's daughter from his other marriage was named after. Their palace or extremely large house and estate had been a museum at one time, but now they had turned it into an armory of sorts, or a type of gun history museum.

Along with our nice apartment came a privacy roof, where we could climb one more flight of stairs to reach the roof which had a very short wall surrounding it. The view from there of Shiraz and the mountains was excellent, and it was always cooler up there, so this is where Mohammad and I liked to go to talk in the evenings.

I was adjusting to Iran, but somehow felt that Iran wasn't adjusting to me. Mohammad's behavior started to change to the point where I began to notice it more and more. He not only acted prejudiced toward the lower class of people, something he had <u>never</u> done before in the States, but also became a mass consumer of all things considered expensive in Iran. If it was new and the hottest thing out there, and expensive, then we had to have it. I didn't like this side of him at all.

He insisted on getting me a woman to attend to my every need, like a live-in caretaker, but I didn't need someone to paint my nails, and brush my hair, or get my bath water ready. However, he seemed to deem this as necessary. In retrospect, I guess if I were honest, I kind of enjoyed it, and I probably took advantage of the situation, too. Now in hind-site, I think the woman was more of a diversion to keep me from being lonely since Mohammad was spending less and less time at home. Again he started acting secretive.

Things went along fine for the first year. By May I had acquired a teaching job as an English instructor, plus I was using my nursing skills to aide Mohammad's mother with the physical therapy she required for being a stroke victim, as well as doing daily checks on her blood pressure. This impressed the family, and made them quite "<u>tanbul</u>," or lazy, since now they did not bother with their three times per week visits, instead opting for telephone calls to replace their presence. That was not the half of it, either.

Mommy Dearest was becoming quite a demanding and offensive mother-in-law, which I thought I'd traded in when I decided to marry a Middle Easterner, rather than an American man. She had made the mistake of thinking I knew nothing about the Farsi language.

I always liked to err on the side of caution, by telling people I knew very little of their culture or language. This allowed me to learn more by listening. Also, if I made a mistake while speaking it was more forgivable. Let's just say she generally irritated me after the initial one or two weeks of pretending to be so happy I was there. It was all an act, of course. After that, almost everything I did was wrong. When I went to the store, I always brought back the wrong <u>type</u> of rice, the wrong brand of milk, things like that. She also would mutter things to me like "<u>shaitan</u>" which means devil or Satan.

At the end of the second semester of teaching the girls English, my students threw me a party at one girl's house, her name was Nada Mahmadyzadk. They insisted I come and kept giving me gifts. The closer it got to the end of the semester, the more gifts I received from the students, their parents, and the Superintendent. The only pet peeve my Superintendent had was that I had picked up the habit of smoking, which to me was a whole new experience, since I had never smoked in my life before that; until after arriving in Shiraz. If you move to a strange land, with a mother-in-law who sits at the table doing crossword puzzles and muttering, "Burrow gome shaw," which means, "Get lost and don't come back," while staring at you to see your reaction – let's see if you don't start trying new things as a way to cope.

As I was saying, my students were wonderful, caring, and very generous, not to mention tolerant and patient. We were both learning a lot about the English language together and I always looked forward to my classes. It didn't take long for me to become the most requested instructor in Shiraz. I was now getting outside contracts with companies to teach their employees English, as well as holding private classes at home. The bond I had established with my students was something very special, and only a teacher in a foreign country can empathize with me here. When I began teaching at Zabanamoozan Language Institute, I did not know Farsi or Arabic that well. Yet, the Principal, despite all my complaining to teach a higher level of student – since they would at least be familiar with some English – instead, put me smack dab in Intro A . . . which is the beginning level.

That first day was a learning experience for me as well. The school gave me a three day training course, but this wasn't long enough, I felt, to prepare someone who had never taught before, how to teach students who don't know your language. We got through the first day, getting to know each other's names, and discussing what each girl knew. Or thought she knew in English. I never laughed so hard in my life as I did that first day.

The most common statement was, "I know Englissi, let me count, 1, 2, 3, 4, 7, 8, 12," or, "I know Englissi, this is the alphabet, A, B, C, D, G, H J, E . . ." And to this day, people on the streets who want to impress an American, will recite similar statements as those above. I just thank God that for those who recited it, I had the good grace of not laughing in their faces, for this would have discouraged them.

I worked at the Zabanamoozan Language Institute and taught on a daily basis. I usually taught from 8:00 a.m. to 4:00 p.m., with classes lasting one and a half hours, then I had a half hour to prepare for the next class. I worked Saturday through Thursday. Fridays are considered their holy day, so we didn't work on that day.

I learned the first day of teaching that everyone's reasons for wanting to learn English was that it is considered a universal language . . . this, and their parents made them come to class to learn it. In Iran it is a symbol of wealth and prestige for a child to attend classes in English. These classes are not offered in the public schools, nor do they come very cheap. The icing on the cake, and the reason why my salary was so high, was that it is very rare to actually get an American to teach English. Which common sense will tell you that to learn a language from a native speaker will give you a much better understanding of how the people of that country talk (slang vs. formal), and the phonetics of the pronunciation. If I were Arabic and trying to teach someone English, the words would never be uttered even close to how they are actually pronounced, due to the Arab's thick guttural accent.

So, here I was at my first job in Iran, as an English Instructor. I was only allowed to teach females in these group classes. The average age of the girls I taught were around fifteen to seventeen and some up to twenty-three. As I said, that first day was a bonding moment for us. The students learned to relax with me, and we all laughed at each other's pronunciations, and what we thought the meanings were of some words. Yes, my students were teaching me Farsi at the same time I taught them English. Not by any intent, just when they used comparisons, such as when I said, "Good-bye," they would tell me that in Farsi you say, "Khodafez," (pronounced: ho-dah-fez).

My teaching was going along great. Not only were the students excited about class, but I was learning more grammar rules than I'd ever mastered in American schools in English. I barely knew the difference between a Noun and a Verb. Now I can proudly tell you what the subject is or the object is of a sentence, as well as the name for every word in the sentence.

Something else came out of these classes too, we were not only bonding on a student/teacher level, but as females as well. Females who were oppressed and made to be silent. Ones who thought they had no rights, which caused them to admire me, an American, who had enjoyed all the freedoms that Americans do, and particularly American women. But more importantly, one who would be returning to that freedom someday.

I really felt empathy for my students, and they also knew what they told me, stayed within the confines of that room . . . which gave us a lot of leeway to discuss things. The English classes turned into two hour sessions rather than the hour and a half they used to be. The students thought two hours would be better for learning. What they really had in mind was more time to learn about life in America.

This was okay, though we still talked and had our discussions in English, and as long as we got through the day's lessons, we had the rest of the time for free discussion.

Every girl couldn't wait to talk about what she had on her mind for the week, and pretty soon we were gathered in a circle in the room, talking about relationships, how women could dress in the USA, and how we were totally free to discuss things with men and disagree on any subject. It always amazed me how the students soaked up this information, like they were learning about aliens from another planet, and had a live species right there in front of them.

Well, two hours didn't satisfy the girls after a while. I had become so talked about, and so popular, that the class sizes were exceeding the capability of trying to teach productively. It went from six classes a week to twenty-four. Then I started teaching privately at home in the evenings on a two hour basis. This type of private teaching brought in a much higher salary . . . and pretty soon, I had no hours open and had to start a waiting list. My classes lasted until 10:00 in the evening. I taught mostly women at first, then brothers and sisters came together. But to my surprise, my husband allowed me to teach men one on one, since there was always someone present in the home, like my mother-in-law. Many of the men students were preparing to take the TOEFL test, which means Test of English Fluency Language. They needed to pass this test in order to go to the USA or Canada to attend college on a student visa.

I couldn't believe my popularity, and for me it was not like work, but one big fun discussion. A lot of laughs . . . like when I was teaching them how to say racoon one day, and pronounced it ra – coon. Come to find out the reason the girls were on the floor laughing is because "coon" in Farsi means homosexual. I had just been describing the masked-like shady creature that is a common moocher in America . . . and they loved it. The rewards came from watching these girls go from struggling to say "apple," to level twelve, where they would graduate and take the TOEFL test. I was so proud of them, these were my girls. We had shared information and shared laughs which only we were privy to. They felt comfortable in knowing they could come to me for advice or just to vent, and it would never be repeated to their parents or any other person. This was a new experience for them. I think it was because they could totally trust me, and I wasn't judgmental of them, either. How could I be? My own teenage years were a whole lot wilder than theirs, and I remembered how much I'd needed a trustworthy friend during that time in my life as well.

The breaking point came during June of 2000. Leila, one of my students, had been caught with a man she was not married to. Her parents, who had aspirations of marrying her off to some wealthy man, were crushed.

Her punishment was to be drowned in the backyard pool by her father for disgracing the family. I couldn't handle this. I wanted to intervene so badly. But to intervene in this type of personal matter could mean imprisonment for myself. She was only about fifteen or sixteen years old, just a girl, and though I didn't see it take place, I heard through the grapevine that her father's sentence had been carried out. I quit teaching young girls soon after, but I think it was more due to the depression which set in after finding out just how Islamic and male dominated this country was.

The way these people saw reality was not the same as my own reality. Since I lived better than most Iranians, and although my husband had changed dramatically since arriving in Iran, and had started physically abusing me, I still never thought of the possibility that he or any family member would <u>kill</u> me for disgracing the family.

I was so shocked something like it could happen in this day and age, therefore, I quit teaching at the Zabanamoozan school afterward. However I continued to teach English, but only to adults. I didn't want to become bonded with the girls, just to see them treated in this manner. And there was nothing I could do or say to help them, or change the facts. So my Principal started advertising my services to go into businesses and teach their employees English.

The first company to contact my supervisor was The Agriculture Bank, which to my knowledge, had offered to pay me the sum of 9,500 Tomans per hour. My supervisor only offered me 4,500 Tomans per hour, which was still quite more than what I'd been receiving before, but also gave him a profit from the classes, as well as any extra on the side. I guess he thought he could get away with this, since he and my husband were old friends from Delta College back in 1979. Needless to say, upon my interview with the school prior to becoming employed, the hubby and supervisor hugged almost like long lost lovers. I wasn't sure if Bijan, the supervisor's name, would hold this connection for, or against me.

There have been people who were loving and sentimental upon seeing Mohammad back in Shiraz, but once our backs were turned, I'd hear Mohammad on the phone telling someone to "fuck this guy where it hurt him the most." So, I was always in a fog as to the affairs of these long lost friends or possible foes of Mohammad Forouzandeh. As a footnote here, I spelled Forouzandeh here with a "u" and not the two "o's" due to this being the original spelling on the Iranian birth certificate (shenas).

But then again, March 5, 1955 is documented as being his original birth date, too. However, back home in America, after Mohammad received his naturalized citizenship, he also changed his name to "Nick" to sound more American. Moreover, he also acquired two more birth dates, as well as social security numbers; one was February 22, 1955, while the other was February 20, 1955. He received his second social security number after receiving the court name-change order. He conveniently went to the Social Security Office and told them he had lost his social security card, then wrote on the application that this was a new application and "slipped" with the birth date once again. I did not understand this at the time, since he had excellent credit and was not wanted by the authorities – at least to my knowledge. Nevertheless, he seemed to be up to a lot of things I wasn't aware of.

CHAPTER 5

Consulting Service

Time went on, I taught English, and eventually had to build a wall of shelves and clean out a storage space in order to showcase the gifts from my student's families. We ended up tearing down part of a wall so my students could see them when they came to visit. It was considered in bad taste if I didn't show off these gifts. If they were not giving me something, then their parents were inviting us over for dinner. Moreover, there is a custom that if someone invites you to their house, it is your duty to reciprocate with an invitation as well. So, we kept quite busy the first year or two.

I want to insert a little bit here about how we lived.

The apartment was only about 1,000 square feet altogether. Which by American standards sounds small for an upperclass residence. But when you realize that most Iranian families live in spaces of only 300 feet or less on average, ours was considered super nice. Mohammad's family owned the apartment outright, so there was no rent to pay. Similar to owning a condo. I think most Iranians had to pay rent on their apartments, unless they had enough money to buy them. Also, our apartment was quite modern by Iranian standards in that we actually had two bathrooms, one the typical Iranian style with the marble tile encased hole in the floor that you squat over, and the other the American style bathroom with a toilet you can sit on and with a bathtub/shower combination. This is a luxury in Iran. The Iranian bathrooms usually had a tile shower but there was no enclosure to keep the water from going everywhere. They were pretty much open, and the whole bathroom floor would fill with about two inches of water, up to your ankles. The drain was slow, so the water didn't run off at the same rate as it sprayed out. We had vertical blinds on the windows and plush carpets. The kitchen stoves were fueled by gas. I never saw an electric stove. There may have been some. We only had a washing machine, no dryer, as washers again are another luxury. It was probably because most dryers and electric stoves require a higher voltage to operate and these apartments were not wired for this. But our washer was a good one and spun most of the water out of the clothes. I would then hang the clothes out to dry. There was a balcony off the bathrooms and this is where we hung our clothes. Ours was enclosed for privacy with shades around it, but most of them were open. When the clothes were dry, I would have to hit them with a broom to get the cockroaches out before I brought them inside.

Which brings me to another point. The roaches there are <u>huge</u>, much like the Madagascar hissing cockroach. Some of these roaches hissed at us as well. They can also fly! I can understand now why many of the women wore scarves over their faces as well, because when you go out at night to walk, the roaches fly right into you. I kept getting hit in the head with them. This is why I had such a phobia about the roaches there. One time I hopped into a pair of jeans that had three roaches in them and I nearly went into hysterics. They are everywhere, and it didn't matter how clean you were.

The only thing we didn't have was a dishwasher. No, I take that back, yes we did. Her name was Maddie. This was the woman my husband had hired to help me. For a while she lived-in and slept in the "backroom" that had been partitioned off from the dining room. The same room Mohammad and I slept in when we first arrived. We were able to move into one of the bedrooms after his sister and her husband moved out, which was about three months after our arrival there. I didn't feel comfortable having Maddie draw my bath water and paint my toenails, although she did a better job than I did. But she did clean, although I was so paranoid of the roaches that I always cleaned after her. When you live in a place all your life, like Maddie did in Iran, you tend to start overlooking the daily annoyances, like the cockroaches. They are called "<u>soosk</u>" in Farsi. I tried mostly to direct Maddie toward helping Mohammad's mother. But I soon felt like the place was too crowded. I eventually told Mohammad to have her go home at nights. As time went by, I started giving her days off and sometimes a week at a time. There were moments when I felt like I might never be alone. There was <u>always</u> someone around.

I taught at the Language Institute from about 1998 to 2000. I should bring up here that I received the Teacher of the Year award for 1998 to 1999. I quit the Institute in about June of 2000 which is when Leila was drowned by her father. However, I still taught at home and at some businesses. Also, many of my students from the Institute went on to take private lessons from me at home.

Mohammad was also teaching English on the side, privately to men and boys. In Iran a teacher is not supposed to teach students of the opposite sex. However, he gave me permission to teach some men as long as there was someone else present in the home, usually his mother and Maddie.

Therefore, along with the money we had brought over from the USA from the sale of his car dealerships, we were more than making ends meet. Especially if you consider that the Toman, their paper currency, had an exchange rate of 800 = $1 US, or that 8,000 Rials, their coins, = $1 US. Now the reason that American dollars survive much longer in Iran than in America is because feeding your family for a month in Iran would cost you the equivalency of 30,000 Tomans, (which, by the way, some people don't even make this much in a month. So I'm judging by the way we ate). The American equivalency was only a little over $30. A taxi ride the distance of 15 miles cost about 500 to 1000 Tomans, which is a little less than a dollar to maybe a little over a dollar American. Hopefully this gives you a general idea of the currency and the power of the almighty US dollar in Iran.

Also, if you are American or at least do not resemble an Iranian, store owners and taxi drivers will automatically charge you double, just because they know you can afford it. There is no such thing as fixed prices in Iran. If you are willing to pay it, they will charge you for it. This inspired much of my motivation to learn Farsi. Since my complexion was somewhat dark (olive), combined with the scarf I wore, it pretty much hid my American heritage. Plus having brown eyes didn't hurt either.

Now, getting back to Mohammad and his shady characteristics which had begun to manifest themselves. Mohammad began making several trips to Tehran, as well as some neighboring countries, such as Pakistan, Iraq, and Turkey. I just thought they were trips to present business ventures to people, since I knew his goal was to begin some type of independent business. He wanted to bring his brother Abbas along with his wife, back from the USA so they could live a comfortable life in Shiraz as well.

I must note here that Mohammad and his brother were very close in appearance. However, Abbas only had negative things to say about his brother. Interesting if you ask me, since had it not been for his close brother, and yours truly, filling out the immigration petitions for him, he never would have obtained approval for his wife's visa to enter the USA. This was when it hit me at about the two year mark while living in Shiraz. I had seen all these ads for Immigration Consultants and heard of people paying big bucks to employ one to assist them with the paperwork, and mock interviews to help expedite them in getting approved for visas. Therefore, I started using the Internet Café and learning about computers.

I started searching for information on Immigration Consulting. I learned that one didn't require licensing and anyone who employed the services of a "Consultant" did so at their own risk, as there was no action or recourse to follow if the consultant screwed up. Well, I could handle that, especially the screwing up part. Seriously, though, I made copies of everything I found, and Mohammad usually either sent a car, or came to the Café to pick me up. Usually if he did the latter, it was a cause of celebration by the employees, since they idolized his humor and knowledge of whatever they talked about. It didn't hurt that two-thirds of the employees were women. While he BS'd, I would take advantage of the time to further my PC usage. I tried to look aptly involved in whatever I was searching for and not notice the kisses they threw at him when he entered the kitchenette inside. They would curtly look my way and blush. I didn't feel as popular there.

* * *

After acquiring enough information to convince my spouse we could do this business, and become rather independently wealthy in the process, he bought, or I should say, exchanged our Immigration Consulting Services for one very new and very expensive PC. A Pentium III with a laser color printer and 17-inch monitor, top of the line brands such as Cannon, Samsung, and Intel. At least it was top of the line during this time period, considering how things progress in the computer industry within a matter of months.

I was off on my learning experience of computers, which was pretty much a self-taught course in humility as well as "pissing off Mohammad at all hours of the night" to inform him that I had, in fact, crashed it again. So Mohammad did what any self-preserving hubby would do, he employed the 24/7 services of a computer programmer named Babak.

Now it was Babak's job to run to my aide, be it any time of the day or night, anything to keep Mohammad from being disturbed from his slumber. I used to stay up at night to work, since this was the only time the house was quiet, and without a million relatives, friends, or students there to interrupt me. It also gave me an excuse to sleep in the daytime when most of these well wishers of Mohammad's were usually present. I pretty much learned all the immigration laws, how to interview, and the TOEFL scores that were needed for student visas. I also found out we could charge a whole lot more for K-1 Visas to the USA, which were business visas, and the clients were willing to pay the high cost, too. This really impressed Mohammad.

I had it down to a fine art. The client would call, I would schedule the interview to determine their eligibility, and then we would get the applications together. I collected the client's information, and filled out all the necessary forms. If needed, I'd also consult with a few immigration attorneys I had retained online for any questions I could not find answers to. All of our client's applications were sent to Damascus, Syria, which was the main processing center. Once we mailed their application via DHL, we would receive a letter back with their file number. In order to get their file number, the client had to pay us the remainder of their bill. Moreover, I, being the good business woman I was, wrote up a mission statement and contracts for "L & M CANCONSULTS."

I thought up this name for our business in relation to the first initials of our names, Lori and Mohammad, and since we were mainly doing Canadian immigration applications. The CAN represented Canada, plus the ability to do something, as in, "We CAN do it," then we were the consults. I still don't know if anyone understood the concept behind the name. But again, the skills I had acquired in doing this business were impressive, as well as intimidating to Mohammad, since he hated computers and needed my help to get on AOL IM to talk to his son in the USA. All in all, we had quite a successful business going. We converted the dining room into our office, which was just off the kitchen. Since the living room was quite large, there was plenty of room to move the table in there for dinners.

I even ordered business cards, pens, and envelopes for the clients to store their paperwork in, and everyone likes gifts, so it helped with the PR. Then, of course, there were those student visas which were becoming quite popular, so I found yet another way to make a profit. I started teaching the TOEFL classes. Remember, this stands for the Test of English Fluency Language. I'm proud to say, my students passed with no lower than an 85% ranking. I started adding additional costs to the Immigration Packages by promoting Resume Packages complete with online job searches through Monster.com.ca. This really got Mohammad wired.

Most of the students who I had taught English to became prospective clients for the immigration consulting business, and most of their parents became our best friends, for a while at least. Everyone in Iran tries to get something cheaper, so if it meant kissing up to two people who ran an immigration business in order for their child to have a better chance at being accepted for a visa, then so be it. We had so many clients I couldn't keep the appointments straight. The reason I mention this is because it relates to one of the first times Mohammad actually hit me repeatedly without any later apologies or explanation.

The evening appointments became pretty steady and clients were expected to bring a down payment with them when they came to fill out their applications for visas. These down payments were used by Mohammad to buy drugs cheaper by getting them in bulk ... my theory anyway. Remember, he still had a bad drug habit.

You might be wondering about my own problem about now since I've brought it up here. Because you can't get Vicodin in Iran, I had to pretty much wean myself off it the first few weeks. But lo and behold Mohammad had taught me a new device, how to sniff heroine and Ritalin. They sold Ritalin like candy over there in the drug stores, and the heroine was pure so it really had a kind of lesser "drugging the mind" effect if you can understand that. I could work on it, and function and never act stoned. I didn't really understand it until I came to the states and was told that 90% of the "cut" in heroine is what induces that drugged effect. I felt it only fair to say this because as I said I've always been on something to numb my mind and now a lot of physical abuse so there it is. Judge me if you want!

I specifically remember not scheduling anyone for a Thursday night, since Friday was a Holy day in Iran, and everyone had it off, therefore I thought having a Thursday and Friday off together would be a nice break for both of us. At 7:00 p.m. that Thursday night, someone showed up and said they had an appointment. I assured them they didn't since I was in charge of scheduling. I re-scheduled them for the following week and sent them on their way. Mohammad arrived home about an hour later and wanted to know where our client was. I explained to him I hadn't scheduled any one and sent the man home. He gave me this angry, yet at the same time, fearful look, and called me a "dumb bitch" and proceeded to hit me until the neighbors started banging on the wall. He told me this should serve as a lesson and not to let it happen again. He frantically called the man who I had re-scheduled and arranged to meet him at the coffee shop kitty-corner to our apartment. His last words to the man were, "Make sure you bring the required amount."

He then told me to throw an immigration packet together. I did as I was told, still crying in disbelief through it all. I handed it to him and slammed the door behind him. When I figured enough time had passed for him to reach the end of the drive, I ran out to our bedroom balcony, which faced the street, and yelled in anger, "I hope to hell you die tonight!" This didn't go over too well, but I figured by the time he had met with the client, secured his money and returned home, he would surely be in an apologetic mood.

I slept on the couch that night just to ensure myself of a pity apology when he returned. Well, I read this one wrong. I awoke to someone pulling me on the floor by my hair. Yes, it was Mohammad. He was trying to drag me out of the apartment. He finally made it out the door with me once I awoke and stood up. With his hand still entwined in my hair, he had such a nasty grip that the pain from this alone created tears in my eyes that were uncontrollable. He shoved me out into the hallway and closed the door and locked it. He told me if I wanted to sleep apart from him, then I could truly sleep apart out with the cockroaches. He knew my weakness of being around those outrageously large, dirty bugs, and knew this would scare me more than anything else. Especially at night when they emerged from the roof or the ground under the door and found their way into the hallway, which was where the majority of them hung out. As I have previously mentioned, these roaches were as big as the Madagascar hissing cockroaches, and they flew too. I hated them. Although I never expected Mohammad to leave me out there all night, I still felt like vomiting at the thought. After about an hour of me banging on the door and apologizing, then screaming when one flew into my face, he finally let me in. The deal was we were not to talk about it anymore, I was just to do as he said. I agreed, feeling defeated once more.

We were making American dollars in an economy which was suffering greatly, yet our income surpassed that of most doctors in Iran. Mohammad was continuously amazed at the ideas I came up with to implement profit. The average payment for our services was about 500,000 Tomans, which is roughly $625 American dollars. Then there was the addition of the resume package and the TOEFL classes if the client wanted these as well.

Mohammad would sometimes charge the client more by telling them he needed to cover his travel expenses to Damascus to talk to the immigration people there. This was all bogus, since we did most of the applications by mail. He did this when he wanted someone to cover his travel expenses for one of his mysterious trips. He would sometimes tell the clients he needed extra money to bribe the immigration officials in Syria.

All the while, I was looking for more information on those business trips Mohammad had been making. I eventually learned how to check flight schedules and passenger lists. He left on these trips very sporadically, probably about once a month and usually for just a few days at a time. But one time he was gone for almost two weeks. He blamed it on a friend's mother who had died and he needed to stay and console the friend. Sometimes he told me he was going to Tehran, but I found out later he had actually left the country. Either he would slip and say something, or I would find evidence in his wallet which I searched every night. All I truly found out was that he had booked flights to Afghanistan, Pakistan, and Bangledesh at various times. I only found out about one of his trips because the lady at the airport called and Mohammad wasn't home. He would sometimes use our client's names to get on passenger lists, and use their passports. I tried to find out by using one of my student's pass words to look up the passenger lists. Both she and her sister worked for one of the airlines.

This was fine, until one day I negligently left this up on the screen where my hubby viewed it and got quite nervous. I told him I was checking into fares to the US, but he didn't buy it. He knew his wife and her <u>foozelness</u> so-to-speak, and after that, the profits went up while our relationship went downhill. Mohammad thought I knew much more than I actually did, but I allowed him to continue to believe it. This was to my advantage, or so I thought.

CHAPTER 6

Digressions

B efore I go any further I would like to elucidate on certain
incidents which had happened when I first arrived in Iran.
Some of these events may have had an impact on how I was
viewed outside the family. Or in general, what a nutcase
Mohammad's wife was.

One of the first incidents happened at a wedding party thrown by
a wealthy family. Where etiquette, as well as custom, is seen as very
appropriate, if not demanded. As I've mentioned before, I was the
proverbial animal lover. At this wedding while walking up to the
house, I noticed a quite young lamb tied out by the vehicles and it
looked very frightened. I asked Mohammad if we could just go look
at it. Mohammad, wanting to keep peace with his wife so there
would not be any scenes, obliged. Mohammad walked over to talk to
some people, telling them, I'm sure, about how his ditzy wife liked
animals. Upon seeing the fear in the lamb's eyes, the first thing I did
was feed the lamb some of the salad we had brought to the wedding.
I'd bought this earlier in the day but had some in a plastic-ware
container in my bag and just dipped out a little to feed him. While
watching him eat, I felt a growing sadness. Why must such a young
innocent animal be sacrificed for the sake of some superstition so
two people can be happy for the rest of their lives?

Now, keep in mind I was still new to Iran and did not completely
understand the justifications behind all these animal sacrifices. I still
felt guilty for the one sacrificed upon my arrival to Iran. Cautiously I
untied it, then immediately kicked it in the ass, yelling, "Run Bambi,
run!"

The people who were gathered around Mohammad, as well as
Mohammad himself, had looks on their faces as if the lamb had just
got up and break-danced in front of them. Pure horror, astonishment,
and amazement passed over their faces. Pretty soon everyone heard

about it, but lucky for me the bride understood my compassion, and we were not banned from the wedding. Nevertheless, I could not help my urge to release this poor lost soul from his bondage, and the feeling of impending doom I thought the lamb probably felt.

Now that I look back, maybe I was just transferring my own feelings of doom on to the lamb.

The next incident gained us a bit of notoriety amongst our neighbors on Afifabad Street.

In Iran cats are as common as <u>soosk</u> (cockroaches), and are liked about as much. Nevertheless, I was a definite cat lover, as you probably remember. I always admired them above dogs for their craftiness as well as their stubbornness not to submit to training. I was always drawn to them, I think, because of this.

When we first arrived, I was nearly in seventh heaven due to all the cats I saw wandering the streets. When we took walks at night, it was my personal goal to attract as many as I could. Therefore I would always take food to drop behind me or throw in their direction. I did manage to coerce a few home with me, get them into the bathtub, and entice them to eat as much tuna as they could devour. Mohammad allowed this little hobby of mine for a while, until one of them tore up our leather furniture. But I blamed it on his nephew who was a holy terror, rather than the cat, whom I was sure wouldn't betray her loyalty. But even while I tried to justify it, I knew in the back of my mind the cat was responsible for the damage. After that no cats were allowed near the Foroozandeh household for a while.

This particular cat which tore up our nice new leather sofa, also was responsible for terrorizing Mohammad's mother, which satisfied me to a degree, as I didn't get along with her very well. Since she was now aware that I knew what <u>"burrow gome shaw"</u> meant, and had related the stories of her stating this to me in Mohammad's absence, she was not too happy with her new daughter-in-law. The cat, in turn, would go into her room when she was watching TV and crawl on the bed, looking at my mother-in-law's food. She would try to shoo the cat away, but it would hiss at her. I watched this from the kitchen and nearly rolled on the floor with laughter, until my mother-in-law shouted, "Lori, <u>jan, burrow pesci</u>," which means, Lori dear, make the cat leave. Or something to that effect.

I then called, "Here kitty, kitty, Grandma don't like you in her room." This statement was always followed by her gritting her teeth and calling me a <u>pedersuckte</u>, which means little devil, or shithead. All in all, I think she actually liked the cat, as it was the only entity which give her stubbornness a run for its money.

Eventually, after this cat's check-in time had expired and he was out on the street again, I had found some kittens and convinced Mohammad that if I were to raise a cat from childhood, then I could teach it to not claw the furniture. There are not many vets there who are willing to even see cats, let alone de-claw them. Cats are not viewed as pets in Iran. They are seen more like vultures and pests.

Nevertheless, I was allowed to keep and try to train a Persian kitten into becoming a respectable member of society on Afifabad Street. This kitten was "<u>kheli shaitain</u>," which means very devilish, or satanish, and this is coming from me!

It was adorable, but very <u>foozel</u>, and very <u>gharm</u>, which means warm, to the right individual who held out any type of meat in their hand. He would snuggle up to my leg and ever so impolitely grab the meat out of my hand, or off my plate, or anywhere else he saw food, then run like hell to my bedroom where he knew he would be safe.

Somehow our Norooze goldfish which had been in the family for three years disappeared within one week after "Kitty" moved in. Eventually I got him calmed down and he became somewhat respectable within our household. However, outside was another story. I used to take him on walks with us and carry him under my montou like a baby. When he got too big for me to carry this way, he would ride around my neck. Which Mohammad was not too keen on. So I decided to leash train the cat. And yes, this took a lot of daytime walks without my hubby to accomplish, but got lots of attention by store owners who must have thought I was treating the cat like an Iranian woman who had disobeyed her husband. That is, sometimes I would be dragging him down the street, since he refused the leash, and other times I would spend almost an hour talking to him about how it would be okay if he'd just listen to me. This always brought on well-wishers, or start foozel store shop owners to wondering, what is this crazy American doing with this cat everyday outside during lunch time, dragging it up and down the streets? Nevertheless, my determination did not diminish, but sadly to say, his stubbornness did not diminish either.

In the end, though, it paid off and within a month, I was able to proudly walk my cat at night attached to a leash, with Mohammad on my left and "Kitty" on my right. Mohammad scoffed at this when we embarked on our first walk out with the cat. At first, he didn't think it would ever happen, but upon the fourth night out for a walk, he realized there was no shaking this obsession I had to take the cat. I thought of this cat as my soulmate, a poor lost soul in a strange land, and I, the only one to care for him and talk to him in a language he wasn't familiar with. I had more things in common with "Kitty" than I did with my hubby. Which is probably why Mohammad eventually got rid of it one day while I was teaching. He said it bit his mom for slapping him out of the room. And since I never hit an animal, because I don't believe this is the right way to discipline them, her slap was probably a rude awakening for it, and thus it reacted violently. Something I had always wanted to do to her as well. I always wondered if I would get as lucky as the cat, that is, to bite her hard before being booted out.

The final incident probably changed everyone's opinion on Afifabad Street about the strange American woman who inhabited the Foroozandeh household. One day I was out buying rice for dinner, when I saw a teenage boy throwing rocks up into a tree. I became engrossed and wanted to find out why he was doing this. All too soon I heard a sickening cry and a little ball of fur fell out of the tree. I rushed over to it just as the kid was getting ready to smash its head with a rock. I immediately grabbed the kid's hand and yelled all those vulgar Farsi words Mohammad had decided to teach me.

The kid just gave me a blank look, at first not believing I had grabbed him, and secondly as to why anyone would want to defend a cat. But this was not a full grown cat, it was a baby kitten which had done nothing wrong and barely had its eyes open. How it got up in the tree was a mystery to me. Probably trying to escape its tormentor. But in due time, I managed to persuade the boy to leave it alone with the comparison of Lori threatening to smash his newborn baby brother's head with a rock.

"What is the purpose," I explained, "It has done nothing wrong to you, it was not a doz, (thief) nor was it acting violently or sickly."

The boy had said this was just what he and his friends did to kittens, so they would not get a chance to see adulthood, which would allow more freedom on the streets.

"Freedom for what?" I had to ask. "For more men to parade their wives down the street and hit them in the face if they happened to walk too closely and not the standard five steps behind them? Or the freedom for more soldiers to patrol the streets with machine guns?" And on and on I went. The kid eventually promised never to hurt an innocent kitten again, but said if a cat got out of hand, then it was dead. So we compromised and all was settled. Or so I thought.

That night came a knock on our door, in which the kid's father stood behind it. He was there to settle this matter with my husband. Men settle differences with their wives between the men, and apparently, to my astonishment, men also settled differences that women had with their children in the same manner. As they talked, I could not resist the urge to go defend myself and explain, which I did, ever so matter-of-factly.

At the end of my fifteen minute spiel on animal rights, the man got up and looked at my hubby and me quizzically, then stormed out, yelling some of those vulgar Farsi words I told you about. I thought I had made my point and he could not refute my arguments. After he left, Mohammad filled me in as to the man's stature within Shiraz, as well as on our street. Apparently he was involved in some type of politics, which at the time didn't really mean a whole lot to me, and NO ONE would touch or mutter angry words at any child of his without paying dearly for it. Mohammad explained the consequences, and I arranged a petition in Farsi for all store owners to agree not to harm any "pesci" unless they were threatening, sickly, or unjustifiably and inexcusably committing erroneous acts of thievery. I had originally done this to piss off people, especially the man who had the unruly cat-hating teen. But it backfired in my face. More so in my hubby's.

The store owners had come to affectionately refer to me as the American who should have been Persian, with the heart of "gold." So they all signed my petition and presented it to my hubby with all sorts of remarks of adoration. Apparently, they had seen me more than I cared to notice them watching. They had related stories to my husband about me buying baby clothing on the streets when I happened to notice a homeless mother asking for handouts. I also bought them food, too, but they did not mention this. They related other stories, but out of modesty, I will not divulge these.

But all in all, it led to a total reform on Afifabad Street. I swear that throughout the rest of the city, cats were treated terribly in Shiraz. However, sometimes people would stop us on the street to talk, then say, "Oh, so you're the one married to the American cat-woman of Shiraz!" Which in turn got a disgusted look passed my way, compliments of hubby, who did not appreciate the popularity I was attaining amongst HIS people. There were other incidents as well, but these are a few that led to my newfound fame.

* * *

There were some other incidents which were not so fun, but rather horrifying and stressful. In Iran, almost every car is a potential taxi. All the cars are pretty much the same model, and if you're standing on the sidewalk waiting for a taxi, you usually get in the first one where the driver agrees to what you are willing to pay him, or who charges a standard rate. This is fine, I suppose, but once in a while there exists some lunatics in Iran, just like ones here in the USA. Let me explain first. There are legitimate taxis in Iran, and these are colored green and white and have "Shiraz Taxi" painted on them, along with a phone number. Then there are all the others who are just people who are traveling somewhere within the city, and want to make a couple hundred <u>Tomans</u> in the process. So they offer travelers their services as well.

In all fairness, some of the women had told me of their experiences with weird taxi drivers who tried to kidnap them, but I just sloughed it off, since up until that point nothing dramatic had happened to me.

My first bad experience happened one morning while on my way to work. A blue Peykan picked me up and we agreed upon 600 Tomans to go about seven miles, which in American money would be less than a dollar. When we got to the first stop light where we were supposed to turn, nothing happened. He drove through it without turning, very cool-like. I figured he was just taking a different route. When the second light came and went, I got a little nervous and told him I had never taken this route before.

His reply was, "Just shut up. I will be the one who decides which way we go." I knew then I was in trouble, but rather than getting upset, I started talking very nice to him, telling him how handsome I thought Persian men were compared to American men, and how much smarter they were, too. He bought into it so well that by the third or fourth stop light later, he was so relaxed with me I had the chance to hop out of the car at the stop light and get his license number.

I walked most of the way home, then called Mohammad from a pay phone and he came and picked me up. He, of course, lectured me on the importance of only taking the green and white taxis, and then only get in if they had other people in there too. Never get in a taxi alone! Needless to say, this was nerve wracking, but not half as bad as the next incident.

It was probably a good eight to ten months after the taxi incident when the newspapers were printing stories about people posing as officers in Tehran and pulling over tourists, then robbing them and raping the women. But this was happening in Tehran, a city about twelve hours away, so I really didn't think that in Shiraz we had much to worry about. I had recovered from the first incident and had been taking any taxi I could get if I was running late for class, but I always made sure there were other passengers in the car first. One morning I had a 9:00 a.m. class, and the electrical power, which has a habit of being shut down nightly to conserve electricity, went out at a much unexpected time. Usually it went out from 9:00 p.m. to 1:00 a.m. It went off at the usual time, but apparently went off again sometime after 1:00 a.m. during the night and I had overslept. I woke up at 8:30, ran out the door and caught a taxi right outside the house. No other passengers were in the car, but it was a green and white taxi. Come to find out these weren't harmless either.

We got to Zand Street which is a four lane boulevard through downtown Shiraz and has very few lights, plus lots of speeding traffic. I needed to get out at Bist Metri Street since the school was right on the corner; you could see it from Zand Street. The driver drove right past it, and told me to sit tight, that we would be home in a little while, <u>after we had some fun</u>.

I can't tell you how fast my heart was beating, but I wasn't going to play the same game again, since I didn't think it would work on this man. But something else was in my favor. It was the time of morning when people were rushing off to their shops, so while we didn't come to a complete stop, the driver slowed down to about 20 or 30 mph. This is when I took the opportunity to jump out. I just dove on the ground since I didn't see much point in trying to step out. My montou (outer covering like a long jacket) caught on the inside handle of the door and ripped all to hell. I almost got hit by the car behind us, but thankfully a few cars stopped and the drivers helped me. I was taken back to the school where I told Bijan (the principal) what happened, and he called Mohammad. Bijan told him that from now on the school would pay for a taxi service to pick me up and drop me off. That was certainly nice of him. Bijan was a very caring person, not to mention that I was his top moneymaker for his Language Institute.

So remember, if you ever tour Iran, your safest bet is to take the bus.

* * *

I would like to add that in the midst of all the chaos of trying to get people approved for immigration visas there arose a certain amount of corruptness. Everyone, it seemed, was open to the highest bidder in Iran. You could get away with almost any crime as long as you had enough money to bribe the person in line above you. With this in mind, I thought back to how desperate some parents were to get their children out of Iran. You would hear them fiercely defend the Iranian government while in public, but in private they would do almost anything to ensure their children didn't have to spend the rest of their lives there. What a paradox to me, but I didn't fully understand until the end of my journey there as to why.

I truly thought of Iran as a country with great people, just poor government. No one was ever happy with the government or the Islamic Regime while in the privacy of their own homes, but in public you never heard a derogatory word uttered. You have to understand that looking through my eyes, I saw a much different Iran than the one you see on TV, or the one the native people saw. I was someone who had adjusted my train of thought toward accepting this country due to my other option of going to jail in America. So, my thoughts were that, yes, this is a different country, but people will speak differently and act differently due to traditions and customs. Also, it was a religiously run government as opposed to America where church and state are separated. I expected things to be new and scary, so when anything went well for me it was just another positive thing that I chalked up in favor of the country.

Except for the behavioral changes I'd witnessed happening to my husband, I deemed everything else to be going much better than I expected. It wasn't like that movie about Betty Mahmoodie, which starred Sally Field, Not Without My Daughter. No, I was more than willing to learn the customs and traditions and try to please those around me. After all, I deemed it not only the respectful thing to do, but the least I could do for these people who had graciously accepted me into their country and homes with open arms.

But they accepted me as an American, and along with Americans comes American money, or better yet, ways to convince Americans to help Iranians in getting to Amrika. I guess I never understood the prestige that went along with being an American until one night after class Mohammad and I were walking downtown and window shopping. We stopped in front of a really nice furniture store. After walking in, Mohammad immediately started to speak to me in English. We had been speaking Farsi just prior to this. I looked at him very strange and asked why the sudden change?

Just then the man who owned the store came over to us and had apparently heard our English, and welcomed us and told us to sit. He sent his son into the back to fetch us tea and began trying to speak in English. His first words were, "Amrikan, no?" When any Iranian ends the sentence with "no" it usually means he is making a statement that means yes. His words really meant, so you're an American.

My husband started speaking to him in slow English and the man replied by saying, "I learned Englissi back during the revolution," then he started speaking Farsi, so I figured his English wasn't very good. The night ended with the man giving us a wonderful deal on some furniture after Mohammad explained he had many more Amrikans who were making a visit to Shiraz and would be looking for furniture to buy their relatives when they arrived.

By Amrikans visiting Shiraz, he meant ones who were married to

Iranians. Then the man found out we were immigration consultants and just about fell off his chair to kiss Mohammad's feet. Needless to say the markdown for the furniture now was at about 90% off. We left the store with a nice array of living room furniture to be delivered the next day and an appointment with the man and his son for the next night for immigration services. There were other times I doubted Mohammad's sincerity in helping these people to acquire visas, but no one had complained, so I felt like the business was going okay.

Mohammad also knew of a square in Istanbul, Turkey, where Americans could sell their passports for up to $10,000 to anyone willing to pay it – and there were plenty of people willing to do this. Then the American would go to the State Department and report their visa as lost or stolen and get reissued a new one. This always made me want to write to the President. How could they ever expect to cut down on foreigners illegally entering the USA with all this going on?

I mean, after all, it was Americans who were assisting these people in their endeavors to gain access to the USA. And let's face it, if you have dark eyes and brown hair, I'm sure your passport would be worth much more. Need I explain further?

Also, I noticed that certain Universities or Colleges would sponsor an immigrant to come to America for the right price. I never believed this to be true until we received one hand written note from some administrative head at a major university (I won't divulge which one) stating that if in fact our client did possess the funds which were listed on his application then a deal could be worked out for his approval, in American dollars, no less.

What gets me is that people complain and complain about foreigners entering our country and posing risks, but they fail to see that it's American people who are assisting these foreigners.

CHAPTER 7

Advance Rumors of Attack in the USA

By mid summer of 2000 I was pretty much getting used to being slapped in the face every time I walked near Mohammad's side when in Public. Things had gone downhill when he found out I had been checking up on him. That is, checking his plane schedules, and trying to verify where he had been on his many "business trips."

About this time we had gone on our biannual vacation to Tehran, where we stayed at the Lalleh Hotel. I always went with him on these particular trips because he said I was expected to go, although they never seemed like vacations to me. I wanted to go where everyone else was going, which was Kish, or to the North by the Caspian Sea, but instead, we always got these terrific hotels where Mohammad would bribe the staff with big tips so they kept me entertained and feeling important. Which I can't blame the staffs of these places, they were wonderful. We had our own delivery boy, therefore I had no excuse to leave the hotel when Mohammad was out on one of his "errands" which usually lasted all day.

The delivery boy was funny and I was trying to teach him some English, but I learned all too well, how little a person's character was worth when it came to pissing off my hubby. One night Mohammad had gotten back to the hotel late, and I was downstairs in the lobby, which served a nice cold Ab tolabee; which is ice cold cantaloupe juice. I was playing backgammon with the delivery boy and teaching him English. I had laughed at a joke he told me about the Turks, when Mohammad came in and stood glaring at us. Then he said, "Lori, go up to the room, NOW!"

I did. And I never saw the boy again. I did not ask, and my husband did not tell me anything, but I was informed <u>never</u> to get too friendly with the staff again. This is how controlling Mohammad was. I was kept pretty much in isolation during these trips. And a wife never delved into her husband's business.

One evening while in Tehran, Mohammad told me we were going to have a visitor. I just shrugged it off as yet another stranger that Mohammad would explain was an old friend from high school or college or something. I started to wonder just how big these classes were, since it seemed as if I'd already met the whole graduating class from my husband's school, and then some. While I didn't buy his stories, I learned not to question them. It only gave him another reason to get angry and hit me, which was becoming more and more frequent.

That night while we were in Tehran taking a walk, suddenly a Mercedes Limo, with what seemed like a zillion cars following it, passed us. Mohammad looked at his watch and said, "Shit, we got to get back to the hotel." Of course, I tried to protest, since I hadn't been out of the hotel in three days. We virtually sat in there, ate there, watched TV, and hated each other within the confines of the hotel rooms. Not much different than being at home, except for the room service.

We arrived back at the hotel, I believe around 8:00 p.m., and Mohammad rushed around the room to straighten it up. We had a suite with two bedrooms, I remember. A computer in the room, and its own private dining area. He got upset at the thought of not having his dry-cleaning picked up that day and called the front desk. He basically told them that if they expected us to return on our next visit they should get their <u>tanbul</u> (lazy asses), up there and clean the room. And bring fresh fruit, <u>shirini</u> (sweet pastries), and <u>chi</u> (tea). While he was fussing about the room I sat down and occupied myself with the computer, which was abruptly turned off when he yanked the cord out of the wall. He asked me what the hell I thought I was doing? I told him I didn't want to bother him. He then told me to go change into the dress he'd bought me earlier that day, and to put on my new scarf, and when the guest arrived, to be on my best behavior. I did as he asked.

Now you're probably wondering why I stayed with him this long in Iran, since his behavior was becoming more violent. It's because I thought he would change. Also, whenever I asked him if we could go home to America, he became irate and said it wasn't feasible at the moment. This was always his answer. "It's not feasible at this time."

The last few months I had repeatedly pestered him about returning to America. I was starting to regret my hasty decision to come to Iran. Especially after my husband had become so abusive. But in Iran, the wife has to have her husband's permission to leave the country. So, I was pretty much stuck there until he decided to go back <u>with</u> me, or <u>give permission</u> for me to return on my own. Basically, I was trapped.

But, back to our guest. At exactly 9:00 p.m. there was a knock at our hotel room door. Mohammad answered it, and all I saw from where I was sitting was a turban. I thought he must be a Holy Mullah. Then I heard the man speak to his entourage, who came through the door first. He then clapped his hands and spoke in a firm, but gentle tone. They left. I thought I might like this Mullah. Mohammad said in his sweetest, yet mocking tone, "Lori, jan, <u>be</u>," which means, "Lori, dear, come!" Then he proceeded to introduce me to none other than PRESIDENT KHATAMI. I just about passed out right there, I was so shocked. Mohammad knew what I thought of Khatami, as I never had any qualms about letting my views be known. I even wrote a letter to the editor once in 1998 to the <u>Iran Daily Times</u> when he was elected, about how I disagreed with his tactics. It was published, but severely censored.

I tried to act as graciously as possible, all the time wondering why he would enter a hotel room alone in a Muslim country, with just a woman and her husband present. Wasn't this a lack of security on his behalf? Couldn't he be blamed for any actions which no one could verify if it came down to my word against his? The wheels started turning in my mind, but Mohammad caught on to my thoughts due to my outward shit-eating grin. I went and got us tea, said hello, and listened to Mohammad explain to me what an honor it was for an American, let alone a <u>woman</u> like myself, to meet the president of Iran.

After our first cup of tea, with them mumbling and me staring at his pants, and what looked like a tie on underneath his outer wear, I got overly curious and said, "I thought you weren't supposed to wear ties in Iran if you were Islamic." He then showed me it was <u>not</u> a tie, just what appeared to be, by the pattern of his shirt.

Most of our conversation was small talk. Khatami asked me how I liked Iran and what I thought of the Muslim way of life and what I had learned from it. I couldn't be as truthful as I would have liked in that I actually thought it was terrible how they treated women and how men dominated them and kept them subdued. How women had no rights in these Muslim countries.

I was excited, nervous, and confused all at once. After awhile Mohammad asked me to go downstairs and eat, as they wanted to talk alone. I did as I was told. Later, after our guest was gone, I asked Mohammad how he knew the President, but he would never tell me. Again, he was very evasive and wouldn't give me a direct answer.

* * *

After the Khatami incident, Mohammad's behavior had calmed down somewhat and he bought me several guilt-laden gifts of a diamond and sapphire ring, with earrings to match, and about seven gold chains and a gold watch with a clasp, to wear when teaching. I had been complaining that I needed a watch with an American date so I could remember where everyone in my family was, season wise, holiday wise, and time wise, so he finally gave me one.

I thanked him, but refused to wear all those gold chains, although it is a custom to show off your gold in Iran as a symbol of your husband's love, and wealth, or so Mohammad told me. To me, it was just asking to get robbed, since I had to leave the school at night now. Plus I'd always hated jewelry. I have never been one to say, "Oh honey, I love this ring," or this bracelet, or whatever. I'd rather put it away for safe keeping as a nest egg, if I have to have it at all. Now buy me saffron <u>bastineeay</u>; meaning saffron ice cream, anytime, but not gold.

I loved the Iranian food, and especially loved their ice creams and juices. All the juice places we frequented knew Mohammad and I would come in following my last class at the school, around 9:00 or 10 p.m. And even if they were ready to close, there would always be my favorites waiting, chilled extra cold, be it <u>Ab tolabee</u>, <u>Ab haveeg</u>, or just <u>Shirmoz</u>, it always tasted better when it was extra cold. And for this they received a 100Toman tip for a 50 to 100 Toman drink. Mohammad always over tipped. If the drink was 300 Tomans, he would tip 200 extra. We also had our own taxi service on Afifabad Street which would come and pick me up anytime day or night if I got hungry and needed to run to the other side of town for a sandwich or cigarettes, since I always stayed up late at night. This had been arranged after my last bad experience with the taxi driver, as you might remember, so we hired our own service.

Our taxi bill for these luxuries usually ran about 10,000 Tomans which was roughly $20 a month American. Somehow, Mohammad managed to keep up with all these extras. Not to mention the best videos, not just one or two, but ten of them delivered to our door every Saturday morning, and usually the top releases.

However, everything went downhill about the beginning of 2001. Mohammad at one time was so angry with me that he chased me from rooftop to rooftop after I forgot to don my hejab when his most hated Mullah Uncle came over. I escaped into a door on a roof which had the glass broken out of it. I ran down the stairs, through some people's living room, and out to the front, where two of Mohammad's friends were waiting to take me back home.

It really climaxed after Mohammad beat me almost to death for calling his mother a bitch, but not to her face. I said I didn't care living there any longer, because I didn't appreciate how their family treated me, despite me working my ass off with all the teaching and the Immigration Consulting Service and trying to please them. They treated me like a red-headed step child. I didn't think Mohammad would take it so personally since <u>he</u> always referred to her as a bitch too!

He grabbed the back of my shirt and dragged me into the bedroom, then threw me on the floor, all the while he kept slapping me. I was screaming, hoping someone would come in and stop him. I did hear his mom yell, but it didn't phase him. She probably felt I deserved it, since she didn't like me anyway. I managed to get outside on the balcony off our bedroom and threatened to jump if he didn't stop. He said, "Go ahead. Let me help you," but then he noticed people walking below and staring up at us, so decided against this. He told me in a very nice way to come in and we would talk. He even apologized. I finally went in. Just as I stepped inside the door, he hit me so hard I fell back against the steam-style heater which was attached to the wall, and cracked my head.

I was unconscious for about twenty minutes. When I woke up, his uncle Mohandes was standing over me, and yelling at

Mohammad. He helped me up, then took me to the hospital, where he paid 200,000 Tomans for my X-Rays and treatment. They were reassuring at the hospital when they said, "If she has seizures they won't last long, it's just a side effect of the abrupt blow."

There was another incident after this one which became a real turning point in my relationship with Mohammad, plunging it even further downward, if that were possible, but I find it very hard to talk about and will discuss it a bit later.

* * *

Then came September of 2001, where all the gossip was that Bin Laden would make opium and heroin cheaper than cigarettes, if Iran and the USA kept screwing with him. I didn't know they were doing this to Bin Laden, but Mohammad felt the need to confess this to me one night after he got home in a rarely good mood. He also said there were rumors going around that the USA would be "bombed" on 9/11. He specified September 11th, because of how it correlated with the American distress call for an emergency by dialing 9-1-1. I listened as he emphasized it was only a <u>rumor</u>, and no one knew where, or what would be targeted, but it was going to make history.

Later I snuck out of the room to the phone after he'd nodded off to sleep, and tried to call my parents to warn them. A recording came on and said, "No International calls are being placed at this time due to the heavy volume." Well, this was on <u>September 9th</u>, and I was getting quite nervous about my family's safety. I kept trying to call all day on September 10th, and yes, even the morning of September 11th, but could never get through.

I had asked Mohammad how he knew about 9/11 but his answer was, "It is general knowledge due to the rumor mill." In other words, if you fit in with some click, then you had information. Maybe the fact he knew President Khatami had something to do with this knowledge.

On the morning of September 12th, Mohammad told me to pack our things, we were getting on the next bus to Istanbul! "Why?" I asked. Istanbul was the next bus ride from Tehran and could get us to an airport where we could fly directly to the USA or to Heathrow in London.

He said, "The USA was 'bombed' yesterday morning, and we aren't sticking around for the aftershocks." His fear was that the USA usually lashed out at <u>all</u> middle eastern countries when something like 9/11 happened. After discovering the whereabouts of the so-called "bombing," I was somewhat relieved for my family, but so heavy-hearted for the others who died. We only got very brief news messages about what happened in America, and I never saw a complete newscast. Everything was very censored. Mostly I heard everything second-hand through Mohammad. It wasn't until after I actually got back to the USA several months later that I learned exactly what happened. I personally believe if the CIA were smarter and had better information they could have prevented it. After all, I'd heard about it two days prior and I was no one with influence. I also believe, now in hindsight, there were terrorist cells in Iran who had something to do with it as well. Possibly even the government itself. This is just my gut feelings after what I went through.

I had survivor's guilt, since I thought we could have prevented this if we had really made an effort to listen to these rumors and warn people. I had tried my best to at least warn my family but could never get through to them. If there was such a heavy volume of International calls going through on September 9th and 10th, then there had to be quite a bit of activity and talk going on between the USA and Iran. But then again, I didn't know if <u>everyone else</u> was aware of these <u>rumors,</u> or only a few <u>inside</u> people. I don't know where Mohammad had heard about the so-called rumors. I wish I knew more. Mohammad was very deceptive and secretive during most of our marriage. If I questioned him about anything, or asked for too many details, he got angry, and by then had become very controlling and violent toward me.

However, this was just the tip of the iceberg for me, and things went from bad to even worse.

CHAPTER 8

Taken Captive

On the morning of September 12th, Mohammad and I arrived at the Shiraz bus terminal to catch the bus from Shiraz to Tehran, then planned to go from Tehran to Istanbul where we could take a flight out to Heathrow Airport in London, or some other far away airport where we might get a flight back to the East Coast of the USA. We didn't know at the time that most of the flights to the USA had been cancelled and many airports were shut down due to security risks. At least for many days following the 9/11 incident.

I only knew we were headed home and I was excited because I had been begging Mohammad for several months now to go back to America. Even with all my legal problems still waiting for me, I was willing to risk it just to get back. Especially since he had become so abusive toward me the past year, I wanted desperately to get home, and had thought about divorcing him. But in Iran, and the Muslim culture in particular, divorce was next to impossible. I personally had never met anyone or even heard of anyone who had gotten one. I wanted to divorce him at that point, but my instinct told me to wait until we got home. It is too easy for the man to keep the woman there against their will, forever. Therefore I didn't want to bring up divorce to him. And especially after seeing a public hanging of a woman who was merely <u>accused</u> of adultery (only by her husband's word), it was more important to just survive from day to day. You have to realize that by asking for a divorce from a person like Mohammad, who was already keeping me there against my wishes anyway, would be like asking for a death sentence. Sad to say. My only hope was that he would trust me enough to want to leave the country with me. Which I thought this was the day it was going to happen.

Now you may wonder why Mohammad decided we should take

the bus rather than a flight out of Shiraz. At the time I didn't know if any flights had been cancelled, but I knew you normally had to book them in advance, whereas at the bus terminal it was first come, first served, so we were able to get our tickets easily.

Therefore, I was willing to put up with the long, dusty, twelve hour bus ride to Tehran just to be on our way to America.

Mohammad paid for our bus tickets then showed our American passports. We then went out front to wait with our very limited luggage, and sat down. Just then Mohammad became panicky and handed me an Iranian passport with the name of Ahmed Malekpoor Mansoorkhany's name on it. This individual was an old client of ours and why Mohammad had possession of his passport I couldn't even begin to understand or explain. How come he needed another person's passport besides his own? But he handed it to me and told me to take it and get rid of it.

I asked, "Why?"

He said, "Now isn't the time to ask questions, just do it!" So I took it, got up, and headed toward the ladies restroom.

Suddenly a group of armed guards pulled up in a truck and started putting Mohammad in hand cuffs! I threw the passport behind some desk and ran back outside. I started to ask what was going on. Another convoy-style truck pulled up and a woman and a man got out. Now the woman, she wore a brown military uniform, but wore the scarf or head covering. They looked and sounded more French than Iranian, but they grabbed me and put me in handcuffs as well, then told me it was due to a corrupt business deal, that we had taken money from our clients. I could not imagine what they were talking about, as I had always been fair in dealing with our clients. All I could think of was that Mohammad had done something I was not aware of with our Immigration Consulting business that we'd operated in Shiraz.

Just as a note here, even though I had tried to check up on all the mysterious business trips he'd taken, I never did find out what he was up to. So, I thought this may have had something to do with those trips and his secret meetings. Also, all through our marriage, he was still addicted to heroin, and may have been involved in some kind of bad drug deal. I really don't know the true reason he was being arrested. Nor why I was put in handcuffs as well.

Probably by association.

Mohammad was loaded into a separate vehicle.

When they pushed me into the back of the convoy-type truck and before they pulled the tarp down, they put a blindfold on me. But before being blinded, I could see there were other people in the back of the truck, who were also blindfolded. Some were men and some were women. They appeared well-dressed and didn't seem to come from the poorer population that dominated most of Iran. Since I had no clue about the legal system of Iran, I could only imagine this was it, and how draconian it all was.

Looking back, I have to wonder if someone at the bus terminal had contacted authorities when anyone showed an American passport and was trying to leave the country. I really have no idea.

Some of the guards wore brown uniforms while others wore green ones. Both uniforms were of a military type, though. None of the soldiers had any kind of insignia on their uniforms to identify them by rank like you see in the USA. For example, you can tell a private from a sergeant by their insignia, but these soldiers had nothing like this on their uniforms. There were also no names like you typically see on military uniforms in the USA. The guards avoided eye contact when directing me as to where to sit or what to do. Some spoke broken English, but most did not. I couldn't tell if they were loading other people from the bus terminal, besides me and my husband, who was put in another truck. Some of the soldiers stayed in the back of the truck with us to make sure we didn't try to jump out the back, or take off our blindfolds.

Since I was pretty much in shock at being shackled and blindfolded, then loaded into a truck by armed guards, I wasn't paying that much attention. Everything seemed somewhat surreal, like I was watching it happen outside my body. People's voices sounded like echoes and everyone appeared to be moving in slow motion. I think when you are in shock you often can't distinguish if this is actually happening to you or just to the people around you. I knew there were other people in the truck, but I mostly saw just a bunch of knees and heads. If I had to guess, I think there was probably about twenty people in the back of the truck, give or take a couple.

The ride took quite a long time, I would guess about six hours.

But when you are in shock time seems to stand still. I just remember sitting there feeling like I was in some kind of dreamscape, and even though I was blindfolded, I still maintained mental visions of what was happening, or what possibly could happen. I held out hope that in the end these people would discover I was in fact an American citizen with a valid passport and they would allow me to walk out. Or better yet, would have a plane waiting for me to return to the USA. I couldn't have been more wrong. I had been under some type of false pride thinking that just because I was an American in a foreign country this would allow me all the benefits of the doubt, while at the same time afford me certain privileges as well.

The ride was smooth at times, as smooth as one can expect while riding in the back of a convoy army truck. We were jammed shoulder to shoulder with others we didn't even know. There were times I could feel us going up hill since the truck encountered some difficulties while trying to ascend a hill and I mistakenly took the gunning of the engine as a signal we were slowing down to possibly stop.

I had to go to the bathroom really bad, but knew better than to ask.

About three hours or so into the ride we did stop for a minute or two and I told one of the guards that I had to go. He told me to literally piss in my pants. Well, I didn't. Not just then anyway. That came about two hours later. I couldn't hold it any longer and the sheer relief I felt after doing so was quickly replaced by humiliation and shame at the thought of what the others must have known I did. I was wearing a <u>montou</u>, pronounced mon-tow, which is the long jacket type of covering for women. It is somewhat similar to a raincoat, only not full length, mine wasn't anyway. Since I was wearing one of these I hoped they couldn't really see the wet spot, as I was also wearing jeans underneath, but I'm sure the others could smell the urine. At least I could.

When we finally arrived hours later, I was still uncertain we had reached our destination. I just sat there with my mouth shut and eyes closed under my blindfold. Needless to say, I did a lot of praying while on the ride. A lot of Hail Mary's and a whole lot of Lord's Prayers, not to mention the new Muslim prayers I had learned, which I figured couldn't hurt either, since both religions had the same goals of sort, to treat people decently and to love God above all else.

After a very long ride which consisted of a lot of yelling amongst the guards, and a whole lot of bumps, we were unloaded out of the truck, but not unblinded. When I stepped out of the truck with the assistance of one of the soldiers, I could feel the pressure he exerted on my arm and thought, boy, somebody must really be pissed off at me or Mohammad, since there was no gentleness in the way these soldiers handled us.

When they removed my blindfold I could see the look on everyone's faces and I could tell they did not know why they were here either, and more importantly to me was the fact we were all just about at the same level of fear as well. A few of the others tried talking to one another, but were told to shut up by the guards. They did as they were told, and I just kept my mouth shut for the time being. I saw some young girls between the ages of about seventeen up to around thirty. Then I saw some women who were old enough to be my grandmother. The men all seemed pretty much older, like into their forties or more, but there were a couple of boys. When I say a couple, I don't mean literally. I mean in relation to the crowd as a whole, since I wasn't interested in keeping statistics at the moment. All I can tell you for sure was that a couple of the boys were in their late teens to early twenties as compared to most of the other men there.

I was about thirty-five years old when all of this was taking place, to give you an idea of the age ranges.

There weren't any other trucks besides ours, that I could see, where they were unloading other people. We stood outside something which I can only compare to a rendition of a **Guantanamo** Bay Prisoner camp, only this one existed out in the valley of some mountains I had never seen before. I could see mountains all around us, but I didn't see any houses or blacktop roads, but rather only dirt paths. There were not that many trees around and the camp looked more like a holding place for prisoners.

The ground was both sandy and rocky, but mostly sand. Trees were sparse, but I could see some far off. They sort of looked like pine trees, but I don't think they were. Maybe cedar. The trees that were closer looked like regular shade trees, I don't know what kind, but they looked as though the branches had been blown off, or at least knocked off, more so than usual.

The guns the soldiers carried all looked the same to me, but some had pistol belts on their waists, along with having a machine gun, and there may have been some rifles too. The "French" woman who had been with the driver of our truck did not stay. She left with the truck. There were no other women guards or soldiers. I thought this was strange because in Iran if a female is arrested a woman officer has to be present because females are only allowed to touch other females.

The camp was in the shape of a square with some of the square having a roof and narrow hall while the remaining part was just open with a fence, broken up by another small piece of building, then more fence. Picture the shape of a square, then put a roof along one side of it and the L that connects to that side put a fence around it. A few feet down, put another roof along the L of one side. It was one big fenced-in yard in the middle with no trees, all dirt and little camp sites where there had been fires in the corners near the entrances of the building.

There didn't appear to be any other people in the camp until we arrived. I'm not sure of the exact time we arrived, but it seemed like late afternoon, possibly around 4:00 or 5:00 p.m. I wasn't wearing my watch. There were insects buzzing around which made me think it was close to that time.

I didn't know where we were, but they must have had electricity since there were lights on in the building at night, and there was a phone. The weather was hot, like it always is in Iran, even during their fall or winter season, it is still hot. A little cooler than summer, but still hot! The temperature normally ran somewhere between 90 to 100 degrees daily, and if it dropped to 80 or possibly 70 degrees, then you really noticed the difference. I could be wrong about the temperatures there as this is just a guess coming from a girl from Michigan. I didn't keep tabs on the weather, but I did know when it was hot. Despite the heat, I didn't seem to sweat that much. But I really did sweat on that ride to the camp.

After they took our blindfolds off, they chained us together two by two. There was no rhyme or reason as to who they chose to chain together. The soldiers just started grabbing us and putting one hand in a cuff, along with one ankle, and then attached it to the person closest to us. Some young people were chained to much older people, women to men.

There was no Muslim law being adhered to now. The chains were a little longer than the distance between standard handcuffs. They were more like the distance of belly chains, but nothing was wrapped around our waists. We were just chained hand to hand and foot to foot.

I was lucky enough to be chained to a girl in her mid to late 20s. I later learned her named was Faresh.

I started to speak, but Faresh shook her head and mouthed the word, "No." On occasion she would quickly get some words out to me, like for instance, to let me know she knew English and they would beat us if they caught us talking. We became bonded that first day, mentally – well, and physically too – but the emotional bonding is what held tightest and was most lasting.

We were then led through a square cement hallway, which if you looked at it from the air, you would see a thin outline of a square with a roof on the inside and with barbed wire fencing around it, but there was no shelter inside the yard. We were led through the square roofed part out to the open yard.

This is when I caught sight of the telephone and demanded from one of the guards my right to use the phone. After all, I thought they were still the authorities and had to grant me this right, because I was naive enough to think this was an International right with any legal arrest. Boy was I wrong.

After the guard laughed and said I was crazy and used the English term, "Koo-koo," I proceeded to call him a derogatory name in Farsi.

Much to my surprise came my first realization that these soldiers were not authority figures, or at least not acting on any official basis. The guard laughed as he slapped me and I fell to the ground. Then he kicked me so hard in the head that I still have the boot indentations in the back of my skull. He didn't stop there. He continued to kick me, all the while mocking my words about using the phone. Faresh fell to the ground with me since we were chained together, and covered her head. At some point, whether it was the kicking, or the pain that overtook me, I passed out and managed to escape the horror for a while.

I'm only guessing here, as I couldn't get anyone to tell me much, but those kicks in the head left me unconscious for approximately four hours. When I awoke – and this is no shite – a Pakistani man had put stitches in my head using a tree twig sharpened with a rock, and some thread from his shirt. He had done this after asking a guard if he could. I'm sure the guard must have thought it was okay to let me die from some massive infection secondary to the procedure. Then they wouldn't have to kill me later, plus it would be more of a hideous death for me. Regardless of his reasons, the guard told him to do it and apparently Faresh knew what was happening because she was the one who told me. Had she not told me, I would have never known since feeling my head and checking for injuries was the least of my worries. Getting some answers and out of this place was my priority!

When I finally awoke my endorphins were still so geared up that I couldn't feel the pain. But I was still grateful to the man for help. He didn't speak any language I knew, but I let him know I was grateful for his help. I tried to convey it through my expressions. Faresh had tears in her eyes. I could hear her muttering the words, "Allah Kaleem," which I learned later is a prayer of sorts to say when you are in really <u>big</u> trouble. I started to speak, but Faresh shook her head again and mouthed the word, "no."

I overheard one soldier sarcastically remark to another about the <u>tanbul,</u> meaning lazy, lady who slept half the day away, then they both laughed.

The sun was starting to set behind the mountains and the air began to cool off. When you are used to the Iranian weather, any drop in temperature seems cold to you. I'm sure if you compare it to most desert weather, it usually seems much colder at night. I still had my montou on and still possessed all my clothes, luckily. Yet that first night was complete torture.

I did realize the soldiers were not about to bring out sleeping bags or pillows for our comfort, but some bug spray would have been nice. There were these big black bugs that bit hard, as well as mosquitoes, but thank God, no cockroaches ... at least none I could see.

We slept on the ground and it was very difficult since one of our hands was always attached to the other's hand, so we couldn't use it to put under our heads. So Faresh and I worked out a plan. We laid like an "L" as close as we could. My left hand, which was chained to her right hand, draped on top of hers and she used both of our hands as a pillow. I used my right hand under my head and this worked out fine for the first night. Not that any of us were able to sleep well. It wasn't like we expected room service in the morning.

That first night, I was also very scared since I had seen the soldiers looking at all of us and making hand gestures like our throats would be cut, or our heads chopped off, then they would laugh with one another.

Faresh tried not to look at them, as we all did, but sooner or later your curiosity got the better of you and you had to find out any information you could, even if it meant enduring ridicule while doing so. Then about half way through the night we witnessed the soldiers eating. I'm guessing here, but I would estimate it was about 3:00 a.m. For whatever reason, the soldiers were cooking some meat on an open fire and we could all smell it. There had been a truck pull away not long before this, so I think maybe food had been delivered to them. Either way, I was not hungry nor could I think about food right then. I was too scared, nervous and confused.

I had wanted to vomit several times, but talked myself out of it since I didn't know exactly how long I would be in the clothes I had on. The nausea was probably a result of my head trauma. At first I thought my head injury was inducing the smells, but I swear I could smell chocolate cookies. Maybe the soldiers had those delivered too, but I know they were a comfort food for me when I was younger. While the soldiers were busy eating, Faresh and I managed to very quietly exchange some information. Between quiet whispers and facial gestures we learned of each other's country of origin and that we both had no clue why we were there.

She was from Bahrain, and was put into the camp with her older brother Abbey, and their parents. Her parents were ill and had been in Iran in order to be seen by a specialist. They had been abducted on their way to the airport.

Apparently some Hezebollahs pulled them over and detained them on the side of the road until the convoy showed up. The name, Hezebollah, means literally "Party of God," but I'm not sure exactly who or what they are. In Iran, we referred to them as the people who would stop you in the street and point a machine gun at you, until you completely covered up anything that might be showing, even if it was by accident. They do it a lot to foreigners who don't wear the head covering properly.

Nasreen was another girl in the camp who lay near us. She was also within facial gesturing distance and established a bond with us as well. Nasreen was only about seventeen years old. She could have been older, but she didn't seem to act older than that. I felt more maternal towards her since the look on her face reminded me of a scared animal that was cornered and about to be killed and knew it. She cried a lot, not that I blamed her, but Faresh and I had more of a knack for holding back the tears. I think Faresh and I still had a bit of pride in that we didn't want to let the guards know how really scared we were. Nasreen did not.

Nasreen was part American and part Iranian which enraged the soldiers even more. They called her a traitor to her heritage since it was her mother who was American. I'm guessing, because they referred to her mother as the Big Satan's whore. They constantly verbally abused her the most. As though Nasreen had a <u>choice</u> about who her parents were. To my knowledge she did not have family there in the camp, but then again our speech was limited. That's probably another reason she was so frightened. There was no one there she knew, and being so young, she literally displayed all her fears, no matter how much the soldiers yelled or threatened her. This also could have been why they picked on her more.

I think I might have fooled them for a while, at least I thought so, since I had olive skin, brown eyes and brown hair, and with my scarf on I could have passed for an Iranian. However the incident over the phone might have clued them in as to my heritage.

That first night, after the soldiers finished eating, they took a pipe out from the cement hallway and smoked opium. The only way I knew for sure it was opium was due to smelling it when my husband had smoked it. This and the soldiers' behavior after smoking it. They became much more aggressive with their words and hurtful remarks. One thing I learned that night was just how much animosity these people had against the USA. Now I was really scared I might be killed if they ever found out I was American. I didn't realize it then, but they probably already knew.

When the sun came up the next morning, I had been awake for most of the night, except for when I was unconscious after being kicked in the head. I tried to lie still so Faresh could rest, but after a while I couldn't and apologized profusely with facial gestures.

Faresh's English was better than most, and this, I thought, would be a comfort to me, but we were seldom allowed to talk. So I guess it didn't matter if the person next to me spoke Swahili for all the conversation that didn't take place.

One thing I scoped out and noticed though, I was fortunate to be with another young, strong girl if the opportunity ever presented itself for an escape.

As close as I could tell there were approximately thirty to forty other prisoners in this camp. Possibly as many as fifty. I believe they must have brought more in while I was unconscious, because there were many more people than could have fit in our truck which arrived first. There hadn't been any other trucks unloading prisoners at the same time we were brought into the camp. We really couldn't see any trucks entering or leaving the compound due to the cement structure which blocked our view, but sometimes we could hear them, like when the guards had their meals. There were also more guards than just those who came with our truck, so others had to have been brought in. I think there were around twenty to twenty-five guards there that first night. A few days later on there were as many as twenty-nine, which I counted during times of boredom.

Now, why so many different nationalities in this camp, I didn't know, but there was a variety, such as some from Bahrain, some from Pakistan, Palestine, Afghanistan, and yes, America. From what I overheard, anyone having ties to the USA, or possessing American passports were picked up. For what reasons I still do not know, if I ever will know. But looking back, I'm sure it must have had something to do with the 9/11 incident, though at the time we didn't have much information about it.

However, I'm not sure if all the people in the camp were actually prisoners. There were a few who just didn't have that scared look of hopelessness and desperation like most of us did. I could be wrong and it might have been their faith which made them less scared or worried than I thought they should look. I mean, you kind of get this idea in your head about how people should act under certain circumstances. Not to say they should all cry and wail and tear out their hair. But some didn't have that frightened animal look like most of the others around. I believe some men might have been planted in there to hopefully overhear whispered information which might have been useful to the guards. I learned to speculate at a lot of things in the weeks to come.

They also had the people spread out around the camp, so it was hard to tell exactly how many were there since the building obstructed much of my view of the rest of the yard. I believe there were about twenty-one to twenty-nine guards there at any given time, so they had to have trucked more of them in after I was unconscious. Also, I believe they brought in new ones at certain shift changes so the others could sleep.

Needless to say, the kicks to my head were not the last blows to my humility.

CHAPTER 9

The Rapes Start

That second day nothing was offered to us in the way of food or water and I was becoming somewhat thirsty, probably due to all my sweating while in the back of the convoy truck. A large man with a green uniform and beret on his head addressed the camp in a loud voice and instructed us somewhat as to the rules to follow. In summary, there was to be no talking, no communication whatsoever, or we would be severely punished. No bathroom privileges. We could go in our pants, or at the site where we were positioned. There was to be no touching or hugging of anyone in the camp.

Someone asked about food, a man at the end of the fence was kicked hard in the stomach. Then the soldier muttered something about that taking care of his hunger pangs.

While I was sorry some of the others had to endure pain for asking questions, I felt like I was cheating off them by learning what NOT to ask so I wouldn't be kicked or beaten. Besides, I had already endured one severe beating for asking about the telephone.

Nasreen was taken out of camp that second day by the man in the green beret and some of the soldiers were saying she would get what every American whore deserved. I never expected her to come back. I figured she would be killed. But she did return about four or five hours later with blood seeping from her mouth and walking with a limp. Her crying was to be heard the rest of the day and into the night, but none of us could help her in any way.

By the third day there I started to study the ants, and at the same time had to go to the bathroom in the worst way. I had decided to wait until dark to do so. I tried all day to tell Faresh of my plans, which might seem like a stupid thing to outsiders, but when you are chained to another person that closely, you pretty much like to keep them abreast of things like needing to do a number-two in the same area where you would be sleeping for God-knows how long.

She shrugged her shoulders with tears in her eyes and said she had to go too, so we planned on that night. I know this might seem like a lot of melodramatic planning to you, but Faresh and I had to keep in mind that this could draw bugs, and since we were sleeping outside with no protection, we had to take into account the consequences.

That night came and we went through with our plan, and yes, it did smell, but luckily there wasn't as much embarrassment since many of the camp prisoners had already done the same and the smell blended in. The only difference now was that it was something fresh to draw bugs, which did not make things any easier.

The first week, I was kept around four other girls, one named Nasreen, one named Faresh who I was chained to, and the other girl who was chained to Nasreen; whom I never had a chance to get to know her name. This was because she was one of the first of us to be taken. Approximately four days after sitting in the camp and trying to comprehend the whole situation, they came to get the girl. She looked to be about twenty-one years old.

Five soldiers came, four of them each grabbed a limb and carried her out like some animal. The fifth soldier kept watch on all those around her while pointing his gun at anyone nearby. She started screaming, and the soldier hit her repeatedly in the head with the butt of his gun, which only caused more screaming and crying.

We never heard a gun shot, so we still clung to the hope that she possibly was given her freedom. But no one knew for sure. Maybe her freedom came in the form of death. I do not know, but I did pray for her that night. And we never saw her again.

The third and fourth day became somewhat of a blur as we still had not been given anything to eat or drink. I was feeling very weak, and if I stood up, I felt as though I would pass out. We were praying for rain, but got something better.

A soldier brought out a hose from one side of the camp and another soldier took a hose from the other side of camp. They started spraying us with water.

We were all frantically trying to grab any water we could in our mouths and hands. But what the soldiers were trying to do, and this is just my guess, was to wash away into the ground the smelly fecal matter that was building up in the camp, and to make sure the prisoners got just enough water so they wouldn't die of dehydration.

Now some people might say you can only last a couple of days without water, but I'm sure we didn't get any water until our fourth day there. The water tasted like the best thing I had ever put in my mouth. And even after the soldiers were done spraying us, we still had some puddles of water on the ground which we took advantage of, scooping up the water with our hands and drinking frantically.

Faresh and I noticed we had become somewhat foes in competing for the puddles and almost ended up hating each other's selfishness. We both realized this later on while lying awake that night and trying to discuss it. However, we were suddenly cut off by a rude voice. A soldier then unchained Faresh from me and led her away. I didn't know where they were taking her, although I tried to ask, but was smacked so hard in the mouth I could taste blood.

I lay there for hours with my heart racing, wondering if I should try to escape now that Faresh was unchained from me. But where would I go? I had no idea which direction to go. Also, the soldiers had rifles and machine guns. Could I outrun a bullet? As I looked around, I realized how futile the whole thing was and lay back with a morbid feeling of defeat. During our time thus far, Faresh had let me know that her parents and brother were in the camp as well, and had secretly pointed them out to me. Her parents were much older than I expected. They looked more like her grandparents. They acknowledged us as well with kindhearted smiles. Now how could anybody smile in the face of this horror? Well the real horror had not even begun yet, and there was going to be plenty more to face.

When the soldiers took Faresh away, I heard her mother scream "Allah chera," which means "Why, Allah?" Her mother was immediately silenced by another soldier and there seemed to be extra soldiers positioned around her parents and brother to ensure there would be no chaos caused by them when Faresh was taken away. Eventually Faresh could almost predict when she would be taken away due to the soldiers congregating around her family just prior to her being unchained.

When they brought Faresh back it was night time, I'm not sure what time, since I did manage to nod off for a bit. How long I was out I don't recall. I didn't dream, but all at once I felt my wrist being jerked and yelled in pain. This was, of course, the soldier grabbing the cuffs to chain Faresh back up to me. She was bleeding from her mouth and nose and was shivering. I thought it was due to the cold, and I slipped my mountou off one shoulder, and even though she had to put it on inside out over the cuffs, she was grateful. I had a feeling of what might have happened, but didn't want to ask.

Faresh just sat there with a blank look on her face and every once in a while she would steal a look in her family's direction only to look away with shame on her face. Then she put her face into her lap and quietly cried.

I tried to put a hand on her shoulder to let her know I cared, but she brushed it off. I just sat there and tried to act interested in everything else to make her feel more comfortable, but how could I really do this. Her shirt was torn in front, but she still managed to keep it closed with the few remaining buttons. This in itself answered an internal feeling I had – that they had raped her.

I do not know the name of the terrorist group who had picked us up, but I do know I kept overhearing the soldiers use the word "Khan" repeatedly. I later heard this name on the news when I finally returned to the USA, as a man who was involved in the planning of the terrorist attacks.

* * *

The two other girls and I, and we were not the only females in the camp, were chosen as the soldiers' "toys." This meant that when they got bored, or just for sadistic purposes, they would choose one of us and rape us, all of the soldiers would. Which, if you counted them all, it meant anywhere from twenty to twenty-nine on any given day.

The first time the soldiers came for me, I knew what was going to happen. I had this sudden nauseous feeling in my stomach, and kept watching the ground intently while the soldiers approached me. All I could hear by the time they got to me was my heartbeat within my ears. I felt a sudden jerk on each arm, and a kick to my back, while I was being unchained and dragged away from Faresh.

Yes, this was the only time the chains came off. I did the usual screaming and fighting, although, I knew in the back of my mind this didn't help. There were too many of them, and only one of me. When the first soldier grabbed me, the other two stood back and pointed their guns at me. I knew what was coming.

Somewhere during that first time I was cut on my throat with a knife. It was being held to my neck and I tried to turn away from the soldier's face and the knife caught my throat. To this day although it is not a big scar I spend two hours trying to cover it up due to not wanting to be reminded of this event every time I look in the mirror.

I kept asking the soldiers where in their fucking Qur'an did Allah tell them to do this? Which only angered them more. I got slapped a few times for that. When they took me out of the camp, the men undressed me, but I was expected to cooperate, and all three men took their turn with me. I'd been hit so many times that the pain being inflicted elsewhere was of no significance. I was too busy trying to keep my mouth free of the blood that steadily nauseated me, since we hadn't eaten in four days, either.

After the first three were satisfied that they had humiliated another American, five more soldiers came in and did the same thing. Different tactics, some hit more than others, some even appeared to be ashamed of doing what they were doing. At least this is how I perceived it. I just stared at them, not taking my eyes off them, since I knew from living in Iran that this made men feel uncomfortable in any situation. One soldier eventually tied a sock around my head to blindfold me. This also kept me from staring at them. That was the worst, because I couldn't see if they were planning to kill me when they were done.

In Iran, anal intercourse is quite common, due to the girls wanting to keep their virginal status. So when they get together with a man, anal intercourse is usually the preferred method of sex, until marriage. This also prevents unwanted pregnancies. Therefore, any chance a man has to do it the so-called, "normal" way, i.e. vaginal intercourse, they welcome the opportunity. Therefore most of the rapes were vaginal. But lo and behold there were a few soldiers who were just plain mean. They weren't interested in anything other than humiliating the girl in every way possible. Of course, that's what they usually say about rape, it's not about sex, but more about power and humiliation.

When the guards were finished with me, I was allowed to put my clothes on before being taken back out to the main prison population and shackled next to Faresh once again.

After that first time I never felt the same again – nor did I think I would ever have normal feelings toward a man again. I felt dirty, sick to my stomach and hated the world. But most of all I was questioning my faith. How could a supposed good God or Allah, allow this to happen to us? I had so many questions and probably hated God by the week's end. A lot of the girl's clothes were ripped, showing they had tried hard to fight before being subdued.

After the first week, the guards started having us get on our feet, about three times a day, to walk in a circle around the yard. Then we would stop at a new place and remain there. I'm guessing it was to ensure no one could get too familiar with their area so that escapes would be less likely. Not that escape seemed likely to me with all the guns the guards had. Having us move around also kept our muscles from becoming cramped and atrophied.

I tried hard to recall the last few weeks in Iran with my husband to figure out some potential reason as to why I was being held in the camp. I could not come up with anything other than he was dirty in his business dealings and had kept it from me. Then I started to think that maybe he'd arranged the whole thing to look like he was being taken captive too, but actually was not. I dismissed this idea immediately since this would mean that someone who I had loved with all my heart and soul, and thought I could trust for the past several years, had all been one big facade. In theory this would mean I could never trust another human being again.

But Mohammad had changed a lot since we arrived in Iran. And I had conveniently tried to justify all his abuse since I didn't want to believe he was really this uncaring about me. The biggest incident I had tried to put out of my mind was when he had sold me for a drug debt to a dealer for the week-end and tried to pass it off as my <u>duty</u> to him and a learning experience in discipline.

CHAPTER 10

The Deal

During the long days in the camp, I had a lot of time to think. And in thinking back to that experience, I could barely keep the tears from gushing down in streams. Yes, I was in uncertain territory in a new land, where horrific things were happening. But in no way could I have known ahead of time what exactly would happen when Mohammad eventually committed his biggest act of inhumane treatment to me, his <u>wife</u>. I never thought this could come from the same man who claimed to love me more than life itself.

But while sitting in this horrible prisoner camp, I had plenty of time on my hands to go over the whole ordeal in my mind. This had been pretty much the last straw that broke my heart and destroyed what little love I had left for Mohammad. Despite all the torture and inhumane treatment I went through in this camp, for some reason this incident concerning Mohammad was one of the hardest for me to write about.

Mohammad had been buying drugs, that is, heroin and opium from a man named Abbas. He was much taller and a whole lot bigger than Mohammad in weight and muscle mass, but seemed to have a kind face on him. He was always polite to me and spoke English very well. His routine was to stop by the house every morning and ring the bell and Mohammad would run down to the door, talk for a bit and pay him, I'm guessing, then come galloping upstairs in a much better mood than when he went down.

Now Abbas wasn't Mohammad's only supplier. He also had a guy named Shahram, but the difference was that Mohammad had to go to Shahram's house instead to pick up his drugs. I had gone with him on a couple of occasions at his insistence. For some reason he liked to show me where he bought his drugs, like the time in Saginaw, Michigan when we were attacked by the two black men.

I usually sat out in the car while Mohammed went up to the outside gate which led to a garden in front of a very nice large house. Once there he would ring the bell. However, prior to ringing the bell he went to a side window and knocked. Shahram would open the window and stick his head out to see who it was, then go back inside. Mohammad then returned to ring the bell and the gate would open. Apparently it was electronically controlled from inside.

I usually sat in the car wondering what I'd do if any police showed up. Well, that was easy, since Mohammad had already instructed me to tell them we were lost and getting directions to Eram Gardens. This was a tourist attraction in Shiraz. I was also supposed to only speak English and tell them I didn't speak any Farsi. I didn't know it then, but I was being used as a scapegoat in case anything went wrong.

One time he wanted me to go inside and meet Shahram, but he had told me I was supposed to act extremely sad, try to cry, and tell Shahram my sister had died and about all the money we had to send to the USA for her funeral. I did as I was told. I knew I would get a beating if I refused to cooperate. I guess this was to buy some time for Mohammad for not paying his full drug debt right away. While we were in the house, it surprised me that Shahram lived with his mother and they were the only two living there in this nice large house. Apparently her husband, Shahram's father, had died of opium addiction, just as Mohammad's father had.

As I've mentioned before, drug addiction is quite common in Iran as well as other middle eastern countries. Even though it is against the law as well as against the Muslim religion. Yet this man's mother knew Shahram did heroin in her house, in his bedroom anyway, which was huge enough to be considered most of the house.

While at Shahram's, I saw his mother leave the house in her chador and head for the Mosque. Shahram told us how religious she was and she thought that by keeping up with her prayers and attendance to the Mosque it would somehow get Shahram to change his ways. She was never rude, always very kind and welcoming, and she confused the hell out of me. Why would she let her son do drugs in her house? But I guess her son was a grown man, just as Mohammad was, and they would do what they wanted, even though their own fathers had died from drugs. It didn't seem to matter that they were in the same danger. Somehow it was seeing this situation that made me realize how bad Mohammad's drug addiction was becoming and where a lot of his money was going. Actually our money. Not that we were poor, but I couldn't figure out why he had to lie to buy time in order to pay his drug debt?

The next incident will show just how bad his drug debts were getting.

Back to Abbas, or Uncle Abbas, or Big Brother Abbas, as he liked to refer to himself around me. There came a time while I was living in Iran that was much worse than any other. This was right after Mohammad had beat me senseless for referring to his mother as a bitch. Soon after that I kept trying to devise excuses as to why I needed to return home to the USA. But Mohammad's response was always the same . . . "It's not feasible right now," or "now is not the time," or "wait a month or two when we are more financially able." Considering all the money we made from our consulting business I couldn't figure out why we weren't financially able to travel at any given time. I mean, we had a nice lavish bedroom, complete with a makeup table, queen-sized bed, and the nicest TV set we could purchase in Iran. Along with a movie video collection to die for. It was just that Mohammad had other things going on in his life and didn't want to leave Iran.

Mohammad was also using a lot more drugs during this time.

Whenever we had guests coming over, or a special occasion of dining out with friends at the local pizza parlor, a sense of uncertainty always came over me. I didn't know if I was more nervous due to the people I might be meeting, or because of what I should or shouldn't say to them in the presence of Mohammad. I had once told some new found friends about Mohammad's outstanding score on his citizenship test in the USA and was almost smacked right in front of his friends for doing so. He took me aside and told me to help fix this error, since his friends only knew him to carry an Iranian passport.

Apparently you couldn't possess more than one country's passport, but Mohammad did, and wanted no one to know about it. Therefore I was never certain when my husband might get angry over something. Another thing I didn't know about my husband.

Anyway, I couldn't believe all the drugs he was doing and

became worried.

You may think what a hypocrite I was by judging him and becoming worried, especially after I had been addicted to Vicodin in the US after my truck accident. But, I approached Mohammad one night when we were in bed with my concerns about his drug use. At first I tried to make some stupid joke about him turning into a human anteater, then I told him I loved him and wanted him to please cut down on the drugs. He blew a gasket after that. He went on and on with his justifications and I knew enough to just sit there and listen and try not to oppose him.

I knew any other action would result in more physical violence. So I left the subject alone for a while.

Mohammad was becoming more and more irritable and going "out" a lot more. He was out of the house a lot, only being there for clientele appointments and usually dinner, then out again until around 2 a.m. One night I was up watching movies when he came home for dinner. My back had been hurting terribly bad that night. Ever since Mohammad had beat me senseless and threw me against the steam heater, my back problems had increased. That day it was especially bad due to my sudden urge to clean the whole house non-stop. I told Mohammad about my back pain and he immediately called Abbas, his drug dealer. I had taken some pills his mother gave me for pain, but they didn't help and I desperately wanted the pain gone since it was worse than usual.

Mohammad said Abbas had just the stuff for my back and had been an RN in Iran a long time ago and could safely administer an injection for my pain.

When Abbas arrived I was in so much pain I would have welcomed anything at that moment. Abbas had brought a couple friends with him and greeted Mohammad at the door, then was led up to our bedroom where he sat down next to me.

He talked to me in this child-like manner, calling himself Big Brother Abbas, and how he could make all my pain go away and that I would thank him in about twenty minutes. I lay there as he injected some brown fluid into my left antecubital fossa. I was told it was medicine he had obtained from the hospital for his own pain when he was in an auto accident a month ago. I figured at the most it was Demerol or a Morphine type drug. I was wrong. About halfway through the injection I yelled for him to stop because I started to totally fade away and felt so weak I thought I wouldn't have enough strength to even breathe if he continued.

He didn't stop. He just kept telling me to relax. I couldn't fight him, I didn't have enough strength. I laid there for an undeterminable amount of time, drifting in and out while I heard voices coming from the front room. The voices became very loud and aggressive at times, then I would fade out. I eventually made the decision that I was strong enough to get up and see where my husband was. I walked out into the living room and remember vaguely of falling onto the couch, or rather just kneeling there with my knees on the floor and my arms under my head, which was positioned on the couch cushion.

I woke up again when Mohammad was carrying a bag out of the bedroom and I was positioned on the couch with my head in Abbas' lap. He was talking to me, telling me that Big Brother would take care of everything this week-end. It had been a Friday night, so I figured he meant the pain would go away for the week-end.

I drifted off again and awoke in the back seat of Abbas' car. I asked him what was going on? He said something to the fact I would be attending to his needs this week-end while learning some discipline and behavior which would be appropriate for any wife of an Iranian man. In essence, in his own way he was saying he would show me how to be a better wife to Mohammad.

At this time I was so "out of it" I had no idea what was happening, and told him that if Mohammad knew what he was saying he would be dead. His response was, "No, I don't think so, since it was Mohammad's idea." I couldn't believe this, but I was still very tired and drifted off once more.

I awoke later to a type of surreal reality, meaning I was awake but the voices and the sounds around me were like echos and it felt as though I was still in a dream state. I then noticed I was in a bed, but not my own, and had no idea where I was. I screamed Mohammad's name and Abbas appeared at the door. I asked for my husband. Abbas came in and closed the door behind him and gave me another quick injection, stating that Mohammad wanted me to have this before he would see me. I again drifted off, but woke up sometime in the night with Abbas stroking my forehead. I was too scared to ask him what was going on.

He said I was to learn and do as I was told this week-end and everything would be better by Monday morning. I started to cry, but he yelled so loud at me it hurt my head. Then he told me to get undressed.

Needless to say, a sick week-end of being locked in a room in what I believed to be Abbas' house and being raped at intermittent times began. And not only just by Abbas, but by men he brought into the bedroom as well. He told me I was to do as they said and to follow all their directions so I would learn what Iranian men appreciated. I was out of it most of the time due to the drugs, but I suppose I did cooperate after being slapped hard a few times by the various men. Sometimes they slapped me even if I did follow their directions.

Abbas came in between times and threw me a washcloth and towel and told me to go into the bathroom and wash up, or he would do it for me. Of course, I did obey. Everything seemed to be happening to someone else, like I was just watching it happen from afar. I even tried to talk myself into crying just so I could feel the tears and know this was not a dream, but, for whatever reason, I could not cry. I felt numb and on automatic pilot. Obeying orders from a drug addicted sadist. I felt angry and totally disoriented as to time. But as they say, supposedly God never gives you more than you can endure. By this time, unbeknownst to me, it was Sunday and time to return to Mohammad. Abbas drove me home and held my hand all the way to the door until Mohammad opened it with a big smile of relief on his face.

I thought his look of relief was for me, in that I got back home alive. Little did I know his relief was actually due to the debt finally being excused with his wife as the payment of that debt.

I was so hurt and confused by all of this that I literally had thought I went out of my mind and imagined everything. Then one night, just to validate my feelings, I asked Mohammad why he let Abbas take me for the week-end and was he aware of what happened there? This time though, I was able to cry and almost couldn't stop when he responded that, "Sometimes you have to do what you have to do to survive. Use all your resources," as he put it.

After that incident I quit feeling any love at all for him, and by this time there had been very little love left for Mohammad since the physical abuse had started. But whatever love I had left was tossed out upon hearing him say this. I started acting almost mechanically until I could figure a way to get out of Iran.

About a month later I decided to try a new plan. I knew he liked my parents a lot, at least at one time in our relationship, so I decided to play on this. I approached him with tears in my eyes and told him my dad had died and I needed to go home for the funeral.

His reply was his typical cold-hearted one, "I'm sorry, but it's not feasible right now. He is dead, so let go of him."

The next morning the phone rang and to my horror I heard Mohammad saying, "Hello Mary (my mother's name), how's Ray (my father) doing?" Then I heard him say, "Well, that's good to hear. Well, here's Lori then," and he handed me the phone. He kept his hand tightly on my leg with this look on his face that he would kill me when I got off the phone. He stayed right there, so I couldn't even hint at being kept there against my will, though I wanted to go home so badly.

This had all happened in August of 2001, just about a month before September 11th.

The saddest thing about all this, is that Mohammad and I had tried to have a child ever since we were married, but for whatever reason, I could not conceive. It was just about this time I found out I was pregnant.

I had done a home pregnancy test and it was positive. Mohammad was elated. I was excited also, since I thought this would give him trust in me, and he would allow me to go home again.

I knew if I gave birth to his child in Iran, he could take it from me and I would never see it again.

After being picked up by the soldiers and put in the prisoner camp, I bled fiercely after about the third week and I took this to be a spontaneous abortion.

I never told anyone in camp I was pregnant. Mohammad knew, which made even less sense that he would have anything to do with putting me in the camp, since he had wanted a child with me so badly. But either way, I was somewhat relieved when I had what I'm sure was a miscarriage. Everyone just assumed all the blood at that time was due to the continuing rapes. Which probably may have contributed to the miscarriage, as well as the beatings. But I wasn't about to tell anyone the truth. I didn't know what actions would be taken with me, knowing I was pregnant. They already treated us like animals. I didn't want to open up any prospects in these soldiers for some new form of torture.

This was also one of the more painful experiences for me to talk about.

While I was grateful that no child of mine would be born in Iran and forced to endure what I had for the past almost four years, I was also saddened at the loss.

CHAPTER 11

Camp Life

Even though it all seems like a blur to me now, I can still remember the first time I was faced with the dreadful decision to eat a bug, or to starve. Not convinced all that well that bugs would keep me alive anyway, my hesitation was probably normal. At least normal for those who have never been faced with this kind of decision. I noticed one man in the camp who would let mosquitoes bite him three times, then he'd eat them. He tried to convince others that this would replenish the system and provide energy. I didn't buy it since the mosquitoes were only recycling his own blood, but I was willing to eat anything smaller than a cockroach. I suppose we all do certain things to survive and in the end no one can honestly say they are proud of what they have had to do, and I'm no exception to this.

After the first time we got some water, I think everyone felt somewhat better. Not that we were getting it on any regular basis, but there were puddles, even minute ones, on the days we weren't hosed off. The soldiers were apparently using the hoses for something, probably to wash, and the excess water would run in a little stream inside the fence. Despite the urine and feces inside the camp the prisoners were willing to drink whatever came through, since they were so dehydrated. However, we tried to avoid fouling where the water trickled in under the fence.

The fence was a very tall chain link type, with barbed wire at the top. Not your typical curled barbed wire like you see at prisons, just about four to six strands strung on top of the fence. The bottom of the fence looked like it was buried in the ground, and to our good fortune later on, there were also some parts that were nearer the surface of the ground.

Also about the end of the first week, the soldiers started throwing us scraps of food off their plates after they were finished eating.

They would toss it towards us like dogs in a kennel that they didn't want to get too close to. The first time they did this, most of the people just stared at the scraps. I think they were afraid they would get into trouble, but there were a few brave ones who dragged the person they were chained to in order to grab the bits of food. I didn't have the heart to run and drag Faresh with me towards a few measly bits of rice off a soldier's plate. Maybe it was after having the water which gave me more confidence than what I should have had, but Faresh apparently felt the same way, since she didn't jump on her feet and dive towards the few morsels either.

However, when no one got shot for their efforts, then many of the prisoners jumped up and dove at the bits of scraps flung in their direction. Even if it was only a few grains of rice. But by the second week we were both diving for anything we could get, since by then we were literally starving to death. I'd lost a lot of weight and we didn't particularly like the taste of insects. My back was aching a lot due to the weight loss and lack of nutrition as well as sleeping on the ground. But if you remember, my back wasn't in too great of shape to start with due to the truck accident years before.

Earlier in the second week we endured eating our first insect, which was a grasshopper type thing. We didn't think the food scraps, even if we were to scoop up all the rations they threw to us, would ever be enough sustenance to keep any one person alive, let alone roughly fifty prisoners. Therefore we faced reality and decided to do what everyone else had been doing for the last few days, eating bugs.

It's not that we thought we were above anyone else in this respect, it was just our minds telling us that something had to change. Either someone might rescue us, or the soldiers would break down and bring us food. I just kept hoping something would happen, some kind of diversion to keep me from doing what I'd only seen in movies prior to this.

Our decision came after a day of only getting a few tidbits of bread which left us even hungrier than if we had not gotten anything at all. Faresh finally broke down and asked the lady to our left how to catch these bugs and she agreed to help us that night. She also told us not to eat them if they were dead, you <u>had</u> to eat them alive. For some reason their legs gave off a toxin after they were dead.

I still remember that first one ever so well. We caught a few that night and I put one in my mouth and held my nose, then bit down. It was still moving in my mouth, which sort of freaked me out. When I felt a sort of spray of juice after biting down, I quickly chewed a couple more times then swallowed what was left pretty much whole. It tasted very bitter, but had a subtle sweet after taste.

The first time I ate one was due to the pressure to try it, to keep from starving. The second time I actually craved that sweet after taste. It's funny how your mind and body can interact to make you believe something actually tastes good. I probably could have eaten dog shit by then and made my mind believe it was good for me and that it tasted good, too.

By the third week we were still being thrown scraps from whatever the soldiers happened to be eating. We scraped it off the ground just to savor the flavor of real food. There were many times when we couldn't get our hands on any of the scraps, since we all dove and fought for them like rabid dogs. At first I tried to wash the bits of food off in a clean puddle before eating them, but learned quickly if you held it in your hands for too long, someone else would grab it and stuff it in their mouth. Therefore, I had to give up the idea of washing the dirt off the food and do what the others did. Eat it quickly, dirt and all.

It was about this time I decided to start being kind, or softer, so-to-speak, to a particular soldier. One who seemed to be a little more open to kindness than most of the others. He was approximately nineteen to twenty years old and looked like a little boy to me. He didn't appear as hardened as some of the other guards. I smiled at him and acted timid and submissive like one does when they flirt, only I was very careful not to overtly flirt or to be seen by any other soldier, or person in the camp, for that matter. We never knew who might talk or get us in trouble. This soldier was usually there at night. They normally switched guards twice a day, once in the morning and once at sunset. When this happened, the prisoners were made to lie face down on the ground and not looking at anything. This was to ensure that chaos or attempted escapes wouldn't ensue, or that someone didn't get out of hand and try to cause a riot at this particular time. We all feared being shot if someone tried to create a diversion, so we obeyed.

Anyway, this particular guard whom I was attempting to make

eye contact with was very receptive and came and got me one night and took me off to the side. His buddies were laughing, so I'm sure they thought he was just doing his job by treating me inhumanely and cruelly. He asked me where I was from in America. I told him, "Michigan," very quietly, then slipped in that he was much kinder than any of the other guards I had met.

He smiled and stated it was not his job to be kind. I told him regardless of his duties, I appreciated seeing his nice smile each night he was there.

He then started yelling things like, "You're nothing but an American whore," and walked away. He turned around though, and while shaking his raised fist at me, he smiled. I chalked this up to at least a small victory. I had no idea what kind of favors I expected, I just knew it HAD to be beneficial to get close to this guard. During this time we were still enduring the rapes pretty much on a daily basis. Sometimes twice a day when the guards changed shifts. It was their way of degrading the women.

The next night when he walked by, he threw a piece of bread into my lap. Faresh nearly giggled out loud. We sat there and ate it all within seconds. Then I had to quietly hear her guilt trip of how we should have shared it with those around us. I didn't exactly feel the same as she did at the moment, but then again, she wasn't the one making the risky sacrifice of being nice to the guard, either. If she knew what I was trying to do, she never let on.

A couple of days later the same soldier was there again. He ripped the cuffs off me, and pointed his rifle towards my head. I thought for sure he'd gone mad on me. I walked in the direction we all knew the way of – which was out through the cement building to the back where they conducted the gang rapes, or individual rapes, whatever happened to be their pleasure. After I arrived out there, I looked at him with tears in my eyes. He handed me some water.

I almost drowned trying to drink as much as I could out of his thermos. He had to force it out of my hands and told me to slow down. He then handed me some type of meat which was cut up into small pieces and were in a little plastic baggie. When I ate the meat I must have resembled a caveman who just found meat after a long winter. At least this is how I thought I looked. The soldier shook his hands and told me, "Motassefam," (pronounced mow-tah-ahsef-am) which means, I'm sorry. I just looked at him, trying to discern if this was sincerity or mockery. I decided on the sincerity, or at least wanted deeply to believe it. That there was at least one man among this barbaric group who actually had a heart and a conscience and could feel empathy for another human being.

I asked him why we were there. All I was told was that anyone who had ties to the USA after 9/11 were picked up. This meant Americans with family in the USA, or people who were born of Americans and were living in Iran. None of this made sense to me then, nor now, since we were not at war with Iran. Unless there were terrorist cells being hidden in Iran. Or maybe they feared the US would retaliate against all Muslim countries. But I also knew not to question the soldier to the point of anger or feeling uncomfortable.

He ripped my mantou off and said it was necessary, then he returned me to the camp with a full stomach, a trusting heart, and now just wearing my shirt and jeans.

Faresh looked at me, but said nothing. I felt ashamed that I had not saved any meat for her and could not tell her of what I thought to be my good fortune. She would not understand.

One other thing I'd learned all too well in Iran, it is wise in times of crisis not to rely on or trust those you think you can. In times of crisis, people will rat you out in a heartbeat to save their own ass. This is not to say there are no kind, loving, warm people in Iran. It just means that when the choice comes down to them or you, they will choose themselves every time, despite any type of relationship or love they might feel for you. I knew this all too well from my experience with Mohammad. He had no qualms whatsoever of handing me over to his drug dealer if it meant saving his own skin.

I also saw this happen in families who ran into political problems with their kids speaking out against the government. Despite their supposed freedoms, you can get into big trouble if you speak out publicly against the government. Granted, not all families are like this, but I did see many who were. In order to save the family from torture or possible execution, they handed over their rebellious youth. I guess if you had to choose between the possibility of your whole family being executed, versus just one member, then it came down to the survival of the greatest number. Save the most lives and martyr the one. I guess it makes sense in a detached sort of way. As I said, I'd found this to be true with my own husband.

Anyway, it was this kind of thinking that made me distrust everyone and anyone in the camp. I knew that if it came down to them telling on me of what they might have observed take place between the soldier and me in exchange for some leniency, they would do it in a heartbeat. And to be quite honest, if I were in their shoes, I probably would make the same choice. You make these decisions very mechanically when in a situation like this and your life is dependent on certain things.

Although I felt ashamed afterwards of receiving the extra food, I also felt a tad bit victorious, like I might be making some progress towards possibly getting out of there.

The soldier couldn't obviously take me out of the camp every night and feed me or be kind to me, but when more than one soldier came, he was usually with them if I was the one they chose to take out and rape that night, or day. Which in all honesty, made it that much harder for me to bear.

There was no comfort in having someone you knew who was kind to you watching these violent acts take place right there in front of them. If anything, it made me angry at him, although, I knew in all sanity he couldn't stop it or interfere without being reprimanded, or worse, but it still angered me. I felt betrayed once more. God, how idiotic I was to think that some soldier who participated in the rapes of my friends and myself would just suddenly change and be my knight in shining armor after smiling at him a few times.

Several nights later I was once more taken out by him along with another soldier. Only this time Faresh was taken as well. After we got out behind the building, we were given some cucumber slices, old ones, but still great food in my eyes. Faresh was handed some too, and she finished them in no time flat. I think she swallowed them whole.

Then the soldiers started asking us questions about our families in the USA. I guess Faresh had family in the US too, although she was from Bahrain. They asked us questions like, were they wealthy? Were our sisters and brothers married? I kind of had a feel for what they were getting at. I thought they figured we could help them get out of Iran and get their citizenship in America if they determined we had enough clout. I was almost too excited to play this game since I was sure it would lead to an exit from the camp. We answered their questions and ate and drank whatever they handed to us. Then they walked away together, not far away, but far enough to talk so we couldn't hear them. Faresh and I exchanged our thoughts and how we might entice them into letting us go.

But when they returned, they started laughing and asked if all women in America were as eager as us to be men's whores? I wanted to blurt out something to the effect that only those women who were kept prisoners by terrorists and who were trying to escape acted that way, but for once I kept my mouth shut.

I really didn't know what to think. Then they started beating us, hard. They dragged us into the building where our legs were strapped up onto a beam and the soles of our feet were whipped with leather belts and the buckles that were attached to these belts.

When they returned us to the camp and chained us together again, we knew we had been betrayed once again by people we thought we could trust. Never again would I make that mistake, no matter how well a person presented themselves. Which pretty much led to my decision that if I ever got out of there alive, I would never get into another relationship again. I didn't even think becoming friends with another woman would ever happen again, based on all the deceptions that arose while there.

Faresh felt just as embarrassed and ashamed as I did. But I somehow sensed she knew I had carried out my fake sincerity for the soldier longer than I had let on – which made her despise me, I'm sure, for all those times I returned without any leftovers for her. Who could blame her? I didn't.

* * *

The routine was pretty much the same. We stayed awake most of the night, waiting to see if we were going to be killed, while we girls got raped throughout the day.

Now the men were tortured too, but I think it had more to do with questioning by the guards. Some men returned afterward, but sometimes they didn't. Often we would hear gunshots close by. However, many times the gunshots sounded far away and may not have been related to our camp. Maybe there was a firing range out there somewhere. I can't say for sure, because I was so tired and hungry that my mind tended to drift off due to the malnutrition. But I do remember hearing closer gunshots at various times.

Sometimes we could scrape food scraps off the ground in the evening, if the soldiers decided to throw them. We ate insects on the side. We got our thirst quenched at the local puddle if we were lucky enough to have one near us. We got hosed down about every third day.

After the first week, we'd learned when it was safe to speak and when you would get the shit kicked out of you for even attempting sign language. So it did become somewhat routine. This might seem hard for some people to grasp, but let me assure you that almost everything in life can become routine, even when it's inconsistency, it's still a routine of inconsistency. Not that I had become "settled into" or became "comfortable" with this routine to plan the rest of my life around.

My thoughts did not run from day to day, but rather minute to minute. It might seem I'm being altruistic here, but it really made me smile if I noticed we had an unusually uneventful day . . . especially for the other girls. And Faresh in particular. Since I was a mother myself, I knew what her parents must have been going through, to watch in horror as their child was whisked away and to not know if she would return alive each time she was taken.

When she did return, they still had to accept the fact that their daughter had been marred and harmed psychologically and physically more and more each time. And this brutality would more than likely affect the outcome of her future in life. Not that I was thinking too much ahead for my own future, but I did ponder what some of these people might perceive of life if they made it out alive.

Would they view people the same? Was this an event they knew all too well could happen to them? Did they have faith in God, or was it just a hope to get them through their time in this dreadful place? Let's face it, everyone needs hope, and some of us can't make it through one day without the promise of something better to come, if not tomorrow, then next week, or maybe next year, or at least sometime in the near future. It is what keeps us motivated and working towards our personal goals.

I've always had a strong belief in God, but I must confess that the time in this camp sure had me doubting a lot of reasons for our existence here. I started to become somewhat resentful towards anyone who prayed out loud, or even insinuated they kept their faith. This stayed with me even after returning home.

* * *

The first time we were transferred out of our camp, I became so excited I almost giggled out loud. It had been approximately two to three weeks. I didn't have a calendar, so I'm just guessing by about how many days passed. I thought somewhere down deep that this was going to be our ride home. If not back to Shiraz, then surely a holding place until we could arrive there. I never thought about them taking us out to kill all of us, since they could have accomplished it right there, then hosed down the blood.

We were once again instructed to lie on the ground with our faces down in the dirt. Then the soldiers came around to un-cuff us. After blindfolding us, they led us out in groups of four to the trucks. We were told to keep our hands on the person's shoulders in front of us. We did as we were told, afraid of the consequences if we didn't.

The ride in the trucks lasted about ninety minutes this time. When we arrived at destination number two and our blindfolds removed, I thought they had just driven in a circle and brought us back to the same camp. This camp looked exactly like the first one. I was puzzled. Maybe they were having fun with us. Getting our hopes up, only to laugh in our faces. We exited the trucks once more with the rough assistance of the soldiers, and were led through a cement hall again. I saw what I thought to be the same phone as in the first camp, only this time I didn't ask to use it. Never say an old dog can't learn something new.

They handcuffed us together once more and Faresh and I were again chained together, which I thought was strange. I figured they wouldn't want us with the same person in case we were making plans to escape and therefore putting us with someone new would screw up our plans. Apparently they weren't worried about this.

When we walked into the camp yard, I then realized that was <u>not</u> the same camp. Same outdoor scenery, but not the same camp. This one had less trees around it and a lot more rocks. This fence seemed to be electric, although I never touched it to test it. The soldiers were pretty much the same ones, with a few new faces. Same routine as before, we were hosed down, thrown scraps of food, though a whole lot less than before. We had to rely more on whatever insects we could catch. Which were scarce with everyone trying to catch whatever crawled their way. The camp retained a foul odor, a lot more than the previous one. It did appear, though, that we were getting closer to the mountains and away from any type of flat terrain.

I had not had enough to eat to maintain the smallest organism on the food chain, and I figured by then I'd lost close to twenty-five pounds. My back ached a lot, but that was the least of my worries. The new guards who had come into the camp made statements similar to "fresh meat," if you get my drift. So my new worry was how many new ways of torture they would invent for us.

I became so nauseated by the smell of the rice the soldiers were cooking that night that I went through dry heaves. Later Faresh told me I sounded like a cat who had a hairball caught in its throat. To me it sounded hilarious, and I almost laughed out loud, but caught myself just in time. When I had started heaving, one of the soldiers looked our way and yelled something to Faresh, but she just sat there and stared at me.

After I recovered I asked her what was wrong? She said the soldier told her that if she didn't shut me up, SHE would have to kill me, or at least put me out of my misery. I'm not sure which statement she used, to be honest.

But this affected her because she knew that 99% of the time they were serious with their threats, so it was a good thing I stopped soon after.

The first night in our new camp was a lot colder than the last camp, so this told me we were moving higher in elevation with these transfers. I didn't know crap about geography, but I did know the higher you got the colder it was and the less oxygen you had. I was actually freezing that first night. Any other time I would have welcomed shivering, since it was an internal metabolism booster and helped you to lose weight or burn calories. I remembered reading about it in some magazine. But at this time I didn't need to burn off any more calories. I was starving as it was.

Again, you think of strange things when you have too much time on your hands. After thinking this, I kept wondering to myself if I would ever have a sane life again where I could just relax in front of the TV in my pajamas, after returning from a hot shower and fall asleep with the lights on in the living room. What a normal life this picture presented to me at the moment ... while in a setting where you know you won't eat or drink normally, nor go to the bathroom. Just doing those small mundane things seemed like heaven to me then.

That night when the guards were smoking their opium and laughing, I tried to ask Faresh what she missed most about home.

Her reply was, "You must never think about home, you must think about this, this is your life now." She had said it with such force, if not anger, I was sure the guards must have heard.

I put my head down and put my one free hand under my head and said nothing more. I was thinking how Faresh really thought this was going to be "it" for the rest of our lives. Had she heard of horror stories that took place in Iran with similar circumstances? What had been the outcome? I became scared then, and feeling like there was not any hope at all left. In retrospect, I realize now she was surviving the only way she knew how at the time.

Again, the only water we got were from puddles, or once in a while when the soldiers would run a hose over us when they thought we were stinking up their camp. We derived a small bit of moisture from eating a few insects and mosquitoes.

There were no bathroom facilities at this new camp, either. If there were, we weren't allowed to use them. When we couldn't hold it in any longer, we had to urinate or defecate in our pants, or wait until after dark so we could go with some degree of privacy, though there really wasn't any. This only added to our embarrassment and shame. There was no other way. We were treated worse than animals.

We were still kept chained together and not allowed to speak out loud to each other. That is why information about most of the other people was very limited.

CHAPTER 12

The Phone

I still remember the night Faresh and I snuck out to use the phone. The soldiers that day had been in an especially giddy mood, for whatever reason, I have no idea, but there was somewhat of an air of celebration and an easiness that existed. It was right after the soldiers had finished eating and threw us more than the normal proportions of leftovers. After the prisoners scrambled to grab what food they could, the soldiers sat down to smoke their opium. They might have been smoking heroin, for all I knew, but a helicopter had flown in a couple of days before, and I distinctly heard the soldiers using the word "teryak," (pronounced tear-yak) which means opium in Farsi. They also mentioned the word heroin. So, I'm assuming the helicopter came in to drop off more drugs and supplies for the guards.

Anyway, the guards seemed a lot farther away from the door that led through the cement hall where I had seen the phone the day we walked through. Also, when they exited the door, I didn't recall anyone locking it like they usually did, with a key, and always checking it after doing so. I kept my eye on the door, since I deemed this as my only way out, as well as my only link to a civilization I believed once existed out there. Too often my mind refused to believe in any reality beyond what I was experiencing right then and there. So, I kept a watch on the door, like a prisoner who was sentenced to death and waiting for a last minute phone call from the governor stating not to go through with it, an appeal had been upheld. I'd always thought, for whatever reason, if anything could stop this insanity, it might come from a phone call within that little hallway.

When the soldiers appeared not to be paying any particular attention to us and were joyously celebrating whatever news or new drug they had at the moment, I told Faresh in my lowest, most serious voice, "We are going to make a phone call." It was as if she had been reading my mind. There were no objections, no talk, just a simple look and nod of confirmation.

We slowly made our way towards the door scooting along the ground by mere inches at a time, all the while making sure the soldiers didn't notice our position was becoming closer to the door. The other prisoners in the camp saw us, but just attended to their own business. At this point in time, no one cared if one of us tried to escape, in fact we would be genuinely happy for them if they got away with it.

The closer we got to the door, the farther away and more surreal everything around me appeared to be. I could hear my heart beating in my chest about a million miles an hour, and I could hear Faresh's breath becoming more labored or excited. When I put my hand on the knob and turned it, I heard the soft click of it opening. I half expected everything around us to explode to smithereens. Or at least bells and alarms to go off. I couldn't believe it! The door was unlocked and we had managed to get in there without being seen.

We still didn't talk, because we were not sure if anyone was hiding in there, or happened to be in there, but we just couldn't see them. After all, the hallway was rather long. It followed through the rest of the building, which was a series of L's that encompassed the yard. As I said, if you were to view it from above you would see a big square with a hollow middle, which is the yard. After we got inside the hallway and carefully closed the door behind us, we just sat there in silence for what seemed like years.

We were in shock at getting this far and way too excited at the prospect of being near a communication device that would link us to the outside world . . . which equaled HELP! After a few moments we both cautiously got up and headed toward the phone.

I picked it up and my hands shook so badly I was sure I wouldn't be able to dial. But, who should I dial? Should I call Mohammad's family? Should I call the police? I thought quickly and decided the only safe thing to do was to call an outside operator and get linked to the USA. I knew if I tried the State Department, or Immigration, they would think it was a prank phone call. The only practical option I could see was to call my mom and have her do the work from over there.

I started to dial but couldn't remember if I should dial 011 or 001 as an outside access code for the USA. I found out it was 001, then the area code, then the number. The phone rang once, then twice, and I was getting nervous that no one was there. On the third ring my mother answered with an irritated, "Hello."

I said, "Mom!" Since I had forgotten about the time difference, I couldn't figure out why she was so disturbed. She immediately asked me how I was, but had an air of skepticism in her voice.

I told her quickly to call the State Department, or call the Swiss Embassy in Tehran, Iran, and tell them to get me out of there. I told her I was dying and only weighed about 80 pounds by now. She didn't say anything, and was silent for quite a long time.

While this perplexed me, I was determined to talk to her, yet so grateful just to hear her voice. A familiar voice from my past, someone who loved me and truly cared about my well-being. I clung to the phone like it was the only thing keeping me alive. I just sat there on the cement floor and kept repeating what she needed to do, and that she had to do it quickly. I told her to enlist the help of my sister so she could get the help of her husband, who I was sure more educated about these things than either one of them were.

I could sense worry in my mother's voice, but I also sensed something else which made me a bit uneasy. She sounded somewhat disbelieving, but at this time I had no idea that my brother-in-law, Abbas, who was still living in the USA, had informed her that if anything happened to me, and I didn't return home, it would be due to Mohammad's and mine drug use. This wasn't true, but later I found out his story was to cover Mohammad's ass, who I felt had something to do with putting me in that camp in the first place.

I remember at some point babbling about rumors I'd heard in the camp that America was going to bomb Iran due to them thinking Osama Bin Laden was hiding there.

My mother's response was, "Good, let them do it, and kill him!"

I then screeched in reply, "But Mom, I'm here in Iran," meaning if they bombed Iran, they would be bombing me also. Hello, Mother, your daughter would be bombed too! We laugh about this now that I'm home, but at the time it wasn't the least bit funny. It was very frightening to me since I had no idea if the rumors were true. After all, the early rumors I'd heard of the USA being attacked turned out to be true.

My mother told me she would do what she could, but still sounded skeptical. I told her I didn't want to hang up, because I didn't know if I would ever hear her voice again, let alone see her. I then told her I would probably get into trouble if they caught me on the phone.

Her reply was a calm, "You'd better go, then." I couldn't believe how casually my mother was taking all this, and I was quite worried she wouldn't even try to get me out of there.

Just then, I heard a man's voice which made the skin on the back of my neck prickle. "Ms. Lori and Ms. Faresh!"

It was a soldier and he wasn't very happy at seeing us in there. Then another soldier walked in and a third. We had been caught and I knew we were going to be punished greatly.

The soldier smacked us both so hard it knocked the wind out of me. Then they dragged us away by a combination of our pants and feet to another part of the building that looked like a construction place for horse hurdles. You know, those wood poles horses jump over in shows. They secured our feet into some type of shackle devises with us lying on the floor and our feet strung up in the air.

They began to ask us who we called. I wasn't going to put my family in danger from fanatic Muslims who might be living in the USA. I kept telling them we had only talked to the operator. They slapped our feet with leather belts. I think they were belts, or maybe straps, or something like them. Each time I said it was just the operator, they slapped our feet harder.

My feet hurt so badly that the pain and burning sensation traveled up my legs to my spine. Then they put something on the belts, or maybe just turned them around so the buckles hit our feet.

The first hard slap from this part broke my toes, at least I was certain it did. Faresh was getting hit pretty bad also. And I'm not sure which hurt more, the pain from getting our feet beaten, or the pain of hearing her cries of agony, when she had very little to do with the planning or the action we were being punished for. I could tell our feet were truly getting a work-out when I noticed blood on the boards our feet were strapped to.

When I couldn't stand to hear Faresh's cries any longer, I finally blurted out, "Modar!" Which means Mother. I then told them I had called my mother. They asked where? I said the USA. They hit my feet again even harder, and this time the strap caught my calf as well. They wanted specifics of where in the USA, not just USA, so I told them Detroit, although this was a lie. It was still located in my home state, if they checked upon my background at all.

They continued a few more times with the lashes to our feet, then made us walk back to our site in the camp. My feet hurt so badly it felt like I was walking on ground glass. I trailed a tad bit behind Faresh, and therefore could see her feet, but I couldn't see what damage had been done, since her entire feet seemed to be covered in blood. When we sat down and were finally able to survey the damage, my heart just about dropped into my stomach when I saw the gashes in Faresh's feet.

What a brave girl to endure what she had for me, and to not give out any information to ease her own intensity of pain. I loved her for that. Now I'd truly found out what it meant to love another person for the pain they had endured for me. I just wanted to grab her face and kiss her forehead and rock her in my arms like a baby, all the while telling her, "Thank you."

My own feet were no better off. I could see the cut marks in the bottoms of the souls and in my heels, but by this time I didn't feel my own pain any more. Only the overwhelming pain in my heart and stomach I had for Faresh. Which made me wonder if I would have done the same thing had it been me in her shoes? I'd like to say yes, but I gave in so easily on my own under the torture, that it made me wonder how much I might endure for another.

I was always second guessing my actions. I had seen so many acts of bravery and good-heartedness in this camp, and during this time, it made me proud to be amongst the company I had. Although, at first, it made me angry that people were praying purposefully to Allah out loud after they had been told not to. And this act alone caused everyone in the camp to be punished. It made me wonder if these people were being faithful to their God, or were they only ensuring everyone in the camp would be punished more than they should have been. I'd seen a lot of acts of blind faith, as well, and to this day, it makes me curious about the faith a person holds for their higher power, be it Allah, or God.

Though, everyone needs something to have faith in, for this is what allows us to continue our daily lives. If we had nothing to look forward to, or nothing to cling to, then what would be our purpose for being here? Survival and carrying on of the species might be the most common reason, but this alone is not enough for most humans. I believe we go through stages of recognition. We grow up with what has been instilled in us by our parents. Then we often go on to search out things for ourselves. We ask ourselves, what do we want to have faith in and belief in? Sometimes we go through a period of questioning. Then at one point comes an all-out enlightenment, where we become so geared up and excited at the discoveries we've made and are still experiencing, that we just want to share it with everyone.

After the realization and the excitement dies down, we sometimes go back to questioning why we ever bought it all in the first place. Often the final realization comes when you understand that no matter how much you understand, or realize, it's not going to make a damn bit of difference in the end anyway, so live life to the best of your ability and try to harm as few people around you as possible in the meantime. Now that I've gone off on a tangent and hit you with this tidbit of Lori's Theory on Religion, let me return to the camp life once more. And how my feet became infected.

It was four or five days after having our feet beaten when I noticed our particular area in the camp had more than it's share of flies in our vicinity. I also knew my feet had felt more painful than usual, and my gashes were becoming infected. There was much redness and inflamation around the sores and white puss-like stuff emerged from the gash on my right heel. I was sure gangrene had set in. So much for all my nursing knowledge. I couldn't even figure out what to do with this infection due to not taking a class in college called, "Survival in an Iranian POW Camp, 101."

I didn't know until later, after I got back to the United States, that a person can die from foot wounds. I remember reading about it somewhere. But I did recognize infection and knew if it wasn't treated, it could eventually cause many serious problems including blood poisoning, gangrene and death.

Faresh did a strange thing, though I have no idea what her reasoning was, but she had been saving pieces of bread and anything that possibly might have contained salt. She then began rubbing it on my gashes as well as hers. I had no idea what she was doing, but I was willing to try anything. She would also spread mud in our gashes and around them whenever we happened to get a little water to create the opportunity. Now I had heard of mud-packs, but I wasn't sure how they would work with actual infection.

Despite being a nurse, putting mud or dirt from the ground into an open wound seemed paradoxical to me, since I figured all the germs in the dirt would just further the infection. And who knows, maybe at any other time the results would have been catastrophic, but sure enough, I noticed the reddening and the puss easing up within a couple of days. Maybe all those Enshallahs I had been reciting were working as well.

Enshallahs are something Muslims say when they are in a bad situation, hoping for a good outcome. It means "God Willing." Or if God wants it to be this way, or it will happen and regardless of the outcome, it is always for the best, since Allah willed it that way.

I thought after having my feet beaten and infected, as well as the continued rapes which occurred on a daily basis, and starving till we had to eat insects just to stay alive, that things couldn't get any worse in the camp. I was wrong.

The next part was probably the most brutal time I had while there. If nothing else, it shows how much some human beings can actually separate themselves from others, to the point where any act of brutality can be justified within their own minds.

Douger and I at my BSN graduation in 1995

My son Douglas whom
I refer to lovingly as
"DOUGER".

Douglas my son.
The one who taught me
what unconditional love
was all about.

John and I –
He is the love of my life

My Dad the unsung hero until now

Bandit & Ringo – my 2 good listeners

Cynthia, my friend and confidante' who taught me that friendship can = trust.

My Girls! (My students – Layla is on right)

Mohammad and I the day we celebrated our marriage... or the first day of my descent into hell.

Believe it or not? Story of captivity is rather bizarre

TUE OCT 2 0 2002

Lori Foroozandeh has a difficult time convincing people to believe her story. It is so bizarre.

Decide for yourself what to believe.

Foroozandeh, who now lives near Napoleon, says she suffered horrible cruelty last year while held captive in a shadowy detention camp in Iran.

"I am not doing this because I want people to hate Iran," she said. "I just want everyone to know what can happen."

Foroozandeh, 36, grew up near Clark Lake and had the maiden name of Woodring. She met Iranian-born Mohammad Foroozandeh at Northern Michigan University in 1993 and he became her second husband. They lived in Saginaw.

BRAD FLORY
Opinion

Mr. and Mrs. Foroozandeh were not Saginaw's most upstanding citizens.

Lori developed a strong taste for the painkiller Vicodin, which led to trouble. She was arrested for prescription fraud in 1998, so husband and wife fled to Iran.

There they ran an immigration "consulting service." They helped Iranians get visas to travel to Canada and the United States.

Fast-forward her story to Sept. 11, 2001.

"Mohammad told me to pack our things, we were getting on the next bus to Istanbul (Turkey). He said the U.S. was bombed yesterday and we aren't sticking around for the aftershocks," she said.

At the bus station, she says, armed guards took them away in handcuffs on separate convoy-style trucks. She has not seen Mohammad since.

Foroozandeh says she does not know who took her captive or why. One guard accused her of running "a corrupt business." She suspects Mohammad was into something shady.

After a long drive, Lori says, the truck arrived at a detention camp in the mountains. There, she says, she was beaten severely, nearly starved, raped repeatedly and threatened with death. Another captive was killed and her body set on fire, she says.

She escaped after about six weeks because another captive bribed her way out, Foroozandeh said. She went to Dubai, United Arab Emirates, and flew home Nov. 14.

None of this can be proven. The best I can tell, no one in the federal government knows Foroozandeh's story or is inclined to believe it.

But there is some supporting evidence.

Foroozandeh claims she once sneaked to a telephone at the detention camp and called her mother. Her mother confirms receiving such a call.

A probation officer in Saginaw County says Foroozandeh looked beat up after her return. She served jail time for the old drug charge.

And Human Rights Watch says Iran has a "proliferation" of detention camps run by "clandestine paramilitary forces entirely beyond official oversight."

Foroozandeh says the United States government did nothing to protect or help her. The State Department has no embassy in Iran and has long warned Americans to stay out.

Back home, she has made a minor splash with Iranian exiles on the Internet and wants to write a book.

Told you it was bizarre. Believe it or not.

— Brad Flory's column appears Tuesdays and Thursdays. Call him at 768-4925 or e-mail him at

The only story I would do upon returning from Iran, and you can tell by the title it was written with "CONFIDENCE".

I escape America once more only this time safely and with a "trustworthy" man, "John"

John and I on vacation in Mexico.

John, "Douger" and I...The two best men I have and will ever have, in my life.

119

My Aunt Donna and
Uncle Bud, Donna was
my fairy Godmother who
helped me get it together
when I got married at the
tender age of "15"!

Andrea Thomas MA, LLP,
the best PTSD therapist at
Henry Ford Hospital.
Andrea is surely
in my opinion;
THE ONE PERSON AND
ALSO FRIEND WHO IS
HELPING ME
DEAL WITH MY PTSD!

120

This is our business card that Mohammad and I used in Shiraz to promote our Immigration Consulting business.

Dr. Barkley who is my knight in shining armor not just for helping me but for all the help and care he gives his patients, and the extraordinary time and work he puts into PTSD and non-epileptic seizures

My son Doug and my grandson Tyler.

My son Douger with
those "GAWD"
awful tattoos!

My sister
Lucy whom
I've become
close with
since writing
this book

My niece Melanie
who is Lucy's daughter,
isn't she beautiful?

My sister Lucy's husband Bob (Red), he used to eat my
cheesecakes when I began cooking at approx: age 10 and MY
CHEESECAKES were made with REAL AMERICAN Cheese,
what a guy!

Even visiting Padre Island I found a homeless cat! I always seem to find a connection with cats, and I love them ALL!

Lori's Dad once more, only looking happier in this picture!

My sister Lucy at her HS graduation! We just started talking again and finding out that we never really did HATE EACH OTHER! So obviously she is my FAVORITE SISTER…not to be confused with the one that slept with my husbands!

Johns Mom & Dad (Hinderer), they are both 93 y.o. and still
drive themselves to church...what loyalty and faith...
I love them both dearly!

My adopted mom who loved my brother so much that she
never wanted to succumb to the OBVIOUS!
I guess this is karma, although I do not hate her, feel sorry for
her is more like it!

Dougie my son before
the TATTOOS!!

Melanie my neice
and Luci's
daughter…isn't
she beautiful
guys….and
AVAILABLE☺

My sister Lucy and
her husband Bob
whose nickname is
Red due to his
outrageously red
hair......
or the red hair he
USED TO HAVE!
Now it's gray!

CHAPTER 13

The Rifle Barrel Incident

N ot long after my feet started to heal, one night I felt myself being dragged away from Faresh by the end of my pant legs. I was pulled over rocks, through mud puddles and outside the fence door. I was very frightened, because this usually didn't start until toward the daylight hours. But their Captain was there and wanted to meet the American – the full blooded one – that is.

Once outside the fence, their Captain, who looked like a cross between Saddam and the Ayatollah, told me, "Welcome to my camp and are you being treated well?" I looked at him and started to laugh so hard I thought I'd puke right there. He didn't find this amusing. He smacked me across the face with so much force I felt my ears ringing for the next two days. He said he didn't like smart-ass women, and hated American bitches!

Though I quit laughing after being struck, I continued to keep eye contact, since I knew this made them uncomfortable. He asked me why I thought I was there? I told him I had no idea, since I hadn't committed any crime.

He quickly corrected me, by telling me that being born an American whore was a crime against his humanity. I'm not sure if he knew what <u>he</u> meant. He then told the other soldiers to leave, but I'm sure they weren't far away in case I tried to run. Next he told me to get ready for some real pain he didn't think I would be so quick to dismiss.

He tore off my shirt, which left me my sports bra to live in for the remainder of my stay in the camp. The other soldiers, when they'd raped me before, had at least taken off my clothes, or ordered me to. This Captain just ripped my shirt off me. Then without any warning, he grabbed me and shoved my face in the nearest mud puddle. He yanked my jeans down and had anal intercourse with me while I was trying not to drown in the puddle.

After he finished the intercourse, he flipped me face up, then took a rifle and shoved the barrel of it up my vagina so hard I felt something rip deep inside, due to the sight sticking out at the end of the barrel, I think. I felt a painful stabbing sensation, like my guts were being ripped out.

I also had a fear that the rifle might go off while inside me, either accidentally or maybe on purpose. But what if it went off and he didn't <u>mean</u> for it to? He told me he was going to rid the Americans of this whore, meaning me. It was then I figured he meant to kill me.

Because of the severe pain of this new type of torture, I didn't care at that moment about anything else, but he kept shoving the rifle farther and farther inside me, which I'm sure caused some internal damage. He asked me if this felt as good as the many men I'd fucked in my life.

He just sat there, getting pleasure out of having me in total fear this way. But to add insult to injury he continued to tell me how pathetic I was, and that I was way too ugly for any American man to want me now. He started asking me questions, like, did I want to return to America with only half my face, or half my female anatomy?

Like this was a choice I seriously had to consider.

Since I was in so much pain I finally told him to just shoot me and get it over with . . . then added a derogatory name in Farsi to hopefully drive him to make the decision. He only sat there and laughed. He then gave the rifle one final shove, which felt like it had entered my abdominal cavity and took all my guts with it. He turned me over to have anal intercourse once again, but left the rifle still sticking up inside me.

Next he made me lay there and submit to the other soldiers, all the while with the rifle barrel, which was slowly killing me, still deep inside me. I could see blood puddling on the ground beside me. It looked as though a pig had been butchered. Believe it or not, this gave me some hope that I might bleed to death and escape the hell I was in. I remember how it hurt much worse when the rifle was eventually withdrawn. Probably because the sight had snagged on something inside and tore things up even more. I also recalled learning from my Nursing classes that when something like this happens, it's the withdrawal of the object which can actually cause death, rather than leaving it in place.

After about three or four hours of this torture, he finally dragged me back to the camp by my hair, and left me there to clean up all the blood while wearing nothing but my jeans and a sports bra. I used the closest puddle to wash off what blood I could. I dipped a leg cuff into the water and watched the puddle turn red.

When this happened, I thought of the movie The Ten Commandments when the Nile turned red with blood. Like I said, you have all kinds of weird thoughts at times like this. But the numbness allowed me to disassociate my body from these events to the point it felt like I was watching it all happen from somewhere else. But I noticed they had taken Faresh away, and I knew all too well what she was in for. I cried for her.

Though still somewhat dark, I could seen daylight starting to break over the mountains. After trying to clean up the blood, I put on my damp jeans and lay on the ground.

I must have passed out for a time because when I woke up, I was staring up at the sky and swore I could see the molecules of the air falling into my face. I still had bad cramps, but the bleeding had eased up somewhat. I then heard Faresh saying, "Mustard." They must have brought her back while I'd been passed out.

"Mustard?" I asked in a low voice.

"This is what you need for pain."

I didn't even ask her to explain. I was thrown off by some of her remedies, so I just dismissed this one as another of those old wives tales. Although, when I got back to the USA, I was told that mustard is a good pain reliever for cramp-like pains. Maybe Faresh knew more than I gave her credit for.

This type of torture went on and on, the whole time we were in this camp.

I was continually threatened with acts of removing my limbs with knives, to removing certain anatomical parts with knives as well.

Later, I understood this was all part of their scare tactics, and their method of making us fear them so much that we would eventually become submissive – which a lot of us did.

Even I did. Though I'd constantly been the rebel of the group and had always had a problem with authority as you might remember, I eventually gave in. In my mind, I figured the more we resisted the more pleasure they got out of beating us and torturing us – therefore, if I submitted, then what fun could it be for them to continue? With this rationalizing I hoped the torture would be over that much quicker. Not so.

CHAPTER 14

New Wave of Torture

Not long after a whole new wave of torture started. This was when they started injecting us with heroin in the gums, so no needle marks would be evident. I will never forget the first dose I received. At first the feeling was euphoric, since all my abdominal pain which I had been trying not to think about was finally lifted. But then I got sick and vomited. Since I'd had nothing to eat, I could only produce dry heaves. Which only made the soldiers laugh that much harder. At one point, I thought my stomach was going to come out of my mouth. I was continuously nauseated, and very weak, which is exactly what they wanted. They started using the heroin about the fourth week into our captivity.

Now I know society thinks badly upon heroin. But I have to be honest here and say that with all the torture, and broken bones, it did help to relieve a lot of the pain I was in. I think Faresh felt the same way, not by any verbal admission, but she sure fought much less the second time they came with the needles. They used what looked like the kind of needles used by diabetics to inject insulin. They didn't bother to change needles between injections. They just used the same needles on everyone. Which is why I got an AIDS test immediately upon returning home, besides worry from all the rapes. However, at the time of all these events I never thought twice about AIDS. We were all trying to survive the best we could.

The soldiers were not skilled in the art of injection, and to be honest, I didn't know that having it injected into my gums would effect me so profoundly. But it surely did. Now when I say it was heroin, I'm only guessing here. It's not like the soldiers read us any drug information. But the general consensus, when we could facially communicate and mouth the words, was that it was heroin. Heroin is a largely available drug in Iran and the Middle East, and it is fairly cheap. The liquid was brown at times, but what bothered me were the times I noticed it was clear. Though I figured it probably wasn't going to kill us, since I reasoned, why should they give us their heroin for a week, then kill us? At least in my mind this made sense.

I remember the first time I got injected quite clearly. Faresh and I were waiting to see if we would be taken away for the guard's nightly fun. All of a sudden we were approached by five soldiers. They unchained us. Then two soldiers kept watch on her, while two held me down and the one injected what appeared to be a half full needle of brown fluid. Faresh was screaming and trying to get away as we didn't know what they were trying to do to us. I was screaming too. This didn't make for an easy first injection.

I jerked, the needle bent. They pulled it back out ever so gently, then had another soldier bring them a second full needle. They tried again. This time I was held mainly by the head and arms. When it was over, I immediately started to feel the nausea in my stomach. I knew I was going to puke, but what was I going to vomit up? Grasshopper legs? That thought alone made me even more nauseated. I don't know why people think of the worst possible things when they get sick. Is it a test to see just how sick they can make themselves, or is it something only I do?

I was too sick to scream anymore when they held Faresh down and did the same to her. I felt bad about this afterwards. But when I started vomiting, nothing came up except a putrid bile taste in my mouth, not even enough to spit out. That's how dehydrated I was. Though we got hosed down every few days, we all were pretty much dehydrated most of the time. Because I got sick so fast, I thought they had given us cyanide or strychnine.

I remembered back to those Tylenol incidents years ago when someone put poison in Tylenol capsules and killed several people. The reason I thought of this was because the taste in the back of my mouth was so acidic. It reminded me of a time I had put an aspirin in my mouth but couldn't find anything to wash it down with. That's what this taste mimicked.

I was certain that during all my heaving, I would probably roll over and die. After they injected Faresh, rather than take us out as usual for the rapes, they just chained us back together. I figured with two puking girls, no one wanted anything to do with us.

An hour passed and I didn't die. But for awhile I was so

miserable and sick I wished I would die. Once the nausea passed I started to feel somewhat better. I noticed the constant throbbing in my back which I'd had for a long time from malnutrition had lifted. Also the headache that occurred every time I barely touched the top of my scalp, from when I was kicked in the head. I actually started to feel, to some degree, thankful towards the soldiers for relieving my pain.

I know it sounds ludicrous, but you have to take into account all the beatings, rapes, and tortures, accompanied by all the pain they caused. I still had occasional abdominal pains from when the captain shoved the rifle barrel inside me, as well as head aches from being kicked in the head, and broken toes from getting my feet beaten. Not to mention stomach cramps from dehydration and hunger pangs.

Now that I look back in retrospect, I wonder if something was going on where they had to keep us quiet. Maybe someone was searching the area, and they wanted to keep us quiet for this. Because the injections didn't stop with the women, the men got injections too, but they seemed to take it a whole lot better.

This is not a judgment call, just an observation from a very doped up prisoner. I do know they took a woman and her husband out of camp the first day we got the injections. They never returned, so no one really knew what happened to them. They seemed rather reserved when they walked out chained together. They didn't act frantic, or upset more than usual. But you have to remember that most, if not all, of these people were Muslims. And to die for Allah, no matter in what context, was an honor.

Most of the Muslim people are brainwashed from birth to hate the Big Satan (America), and any type of injury or death that happens to an American which also causes the death of the person inflicting it, is considered an act of martyrdom, if the person is Muslim and carrying it out in the name of Allah. This is why there are so many suicide bombers who try to take out as many of the "enemy" with them as possible. For them it is an honor to die in the name of Allah.

I can understand why some believe this to be true and how they get so caught up in the heroics of martyrdom. This doesn't mean I accept or condone it, it merely means I understand how this mind-set comes about.

The day they gave us the heroin injections, oddly enough the women weren't taken out and accosted in any way. The following day we were roused before sunset, to be given yet another injection. I did fight, but now that I knew what it was, I didn't fight as hard. I think I associated this injection with another day free of the men not raping or torturing us. Or maybe it was just relief from the pain, but either way, they went through the same type of routine once more. However, the soldiers didn't appear to be having as much fun as they had the day before, which was when we got our first injection. I'm sure this was due to the fear factor not existing as much the second time, now that we knew it wasn't poison and actually helped relieve some of our pain. But the guards truly looked like they were carrying out orders of some sort by injecting everyone.

Also that morning they seemed to throw out more food than usual and this time Faresh and I got some. One man went for a "whole" piece of bread, but a Pakistani lady pushed him with all her might to get at it. The man tried to hit her with his unchained hand, but fell down, probably due to the effects of the drug. The lady grabbed the bread and stuffed it all in her mouth, not even sharing it with the person chained to her.

Of course, this was not the first time people fought over food, but it seemed more predominant that day than other days. Probably because we were thrown more than the usual amount. Faresh and I ended up with a few beans we found on the ground. The soldiers had been eating a type of soup common for breakfast in Iran called, "osh," and it consisted of beans, meat, and a few other things to fill you up in the morning.

Some people dipped little pieces of bread they'd recovered onto the ground where the broth from the soup lingered. Faresh and I had no bread that morning, but we were consoled somewhat with the few beans we found.

I didn't even bother to try cleaning them off. I'd quit doing that after the first week. If you held them too long in your hand, whether to wipe them off, or dip them in a nearby puddle of water, the chances of them being swiped out of your hand were pretty good. The soldiers didn't seem to mind when we fought, especially physically. Not that it happened all that often, but it did happen, especially when they threw their tidbits of food out to us. They would just let us go at it, unless it looked like two people were setting up a diversion so others might try to escape. Therefore, while they let it happen, they didn't let it proceed too long.

The second day of injections did not go as well as the first day. My gums were very sore to the touch due to the first needle bending while being injected. Also, the soldiers didn't take another vacation day from their sexual fun with the girls either.

They came and got Faresh first. This left me somewhat thankful. I know it sounds weird, if not downright cold, but you have to put yourself into my shoes. I had been succumbing to this routine for roughly five weeks now, though humiliating and frightening each time, but a routine non the less. And any time you were afforded a little extra time, or at least knowing ahead of time, that something was about to happen, you were somewhat relieved inside. And I was relieved when they took Faresh first.

I had tried rubbing dirt on my sore gum – and don't ask me why I did this – but I thought if my mouth tasted really dirty (no pun intended) then possibly the soldiers would keep their lips off mine. Again this sounds bad, but it happened. There were certain soldiers you knew would use their lips, even if in a rough nature, they still used them, then there were some who didn't. I never understood why anyone would want to use their lips on women who had not brushed their teeth in five weeks, and ate grasshoppers when they became available, not to mention all the eating off the ground we did and the occasional vomiting. But then again, I didn't understand a whole lot lately, and at this point I wasn't trying to figure things out either. I was just trying to survive the best I could under the circumstances.

When they finally come for me and brought Faresh back, I noticed she was not crying. This alone didn't tell me anything, but her lack of facial grimaces did. This in its own way told me they were not trying any new torture methods on us despite the heroin injections being something new they were using. So I was once more relieved. I went with the soldiers, who took their turns with me, then returned me to Faresh where I was handcuffed once more. As I said, it was pretty much a routine.

There were anywhere from twenty to twenty-nine soldiers in the camp and on some days we were forced to endure the company of all twenty-nine. At times when I was bored, I had counted them. I had become so good at detaching myself from what was happening, that any type of scream or command barked by one of the soldiers became an automatic compliance by my body. My mind was usually elsewhere, either counting the clouds in the sky, or thinking about past Christmases in Michigan. It was never there with the soldiers, and this I thought to be my one victory over them.

The soldiers didn't care, they just wanted us for one thing, and that was humiliation. Someone to use their authority and self-appointed power on, who would be scared enough to comply. This only strengthened their views on the people they were most jealous of, which are Americans.

It was obvious that they looked at me with pure disgust and hatred, more so than the others, I think. They wanted, like every other Iranian, to go to America and to escape the society of the IRI (Islamic Republic of Iran), a religiously run society and one with very little tolerance for those who didn't comply to their strict standards. In essence, they had no control in their own society or in their homeland, so-to-speak, probably not even in their own homes, so this was the one place they could vent all their frustrations without getting into trouble.

And how appropriate on people who were either half, or full American, or who had ties to Americans in some way. Something they secretly desired, but projected outwardly only hate towards.

Another week passed and my gums were starting to become abscessed and sore due to the injections. Faresh's gums were bleeding most of the time, and I was surprised mine weren't bleeding as well, since they were so sore. I do believe Faresh had become good at the art of disassociation too, and this is why the soldiers held so much contempt and hatred towards the two of us. We were able to escape without escaping, and they couldn't control this.

After about a week of getting the heroin injections, all of a sudden they stopped giving them to us.

Now the first day they'd given us only one injection and the second day as well. But on the third and fourth days they started giving us two to four injections. Which really made my mind drift off whether I wanted it to or not. Then after a week of these injections, they cut us off cold turkey.

I thought you were supposed to go through months of use to get the benefit of withdrawals, but I have to say that's what those weird feelings were I had. I started getting cold, then hot. I had a sudden urge to lie down and stretch and keep stretching until my body separated at the waist. I don't know if these were true withdrawal symptoms or not, but regardless, they were light ones if they were.

I had a constant thirst which left me licking my skin incessantly for the liquid sweat and sucking on any dirt that even remotely looked wet, besides the hot and cold sensations. I, having the imagination I do, also envisioned me going through menopause in a place like this. At least the hot and cold flashes made me think I might be.

After a couple of days of letting us go through withdrawals, they resumed the injections. Some people obviously went through worse withdrawals, due to the screaming I heard. Then again, I think some of the men who were held in the camp went through withdrawals after that first week or so from their own private habits they had at home. The added torture of the later injections and then cutting them off cold turkey again, I believe made it worse for some of them.

CHAPTER 15

Another New Torture

They eventually started taking us out in twos, so that one of us could watch while the other got tortured. That way we could see exactly what was in store for us next. Therefore, they took Faresh and I out together.

During one of these sessions they gave Faresh a partial episiotomy with a kitchen knife and told her this should loosen her up some since apparently she was so tight.

God that was horrible!

They held her down and used the serrated edge of a <u>butter knife</u> and sawed at her vagina like it was a piece of meat. She was screaming, of course. But one of the soldiers held his hand over her mouth to stifle her screams for the most part. It was sickening. She bled profusely from their horrible operation. This was during one of the times when they weren't giving us the heroin injections, so she felt every bit of the pain. Since I'd had a baby and been married, I guess I was deemed "lose enough" so I wasn't put through the same type of torture she was.

* * *

At one point I was getting good at pretty much passing out after being given an injection, so I would like to think I don't remember much of what happened, but this is a fallacy. Because, still to this day, I wake up from nightmares that remind me all too well of what happened during those times. Like the times they beat our feet with the leather belts.

There were times they had gloves on and said one fist was for the mouth, and the other for . . . . And this was very painful, since, if we moved during the whole ordeal then they were entitled to hit us with their fist ten times. This was only one of their sick games. They gave us orders to not scream, not move, not to shout, or they would retaliate. But even if we didn't scream or move, they still retaliated just to be cruel.

One time two soldiers took me into a shed off to the side of the compound and strung me up to a beam by my wrists. They undressed me, then sat and stared at me for a while, laughing. After awhile they climbed onto a chair to have sex with me. It was memorable because my shoulders hurt like hell.

They loved to generally degrade me, by telling me how bad Americans were, and how we allowed our young girls to be whores and get pregnant. I'm sure they were referring to teenage pregnancies. They talked about how all the American kids were on drugs and had no respect for their elders . . . which is a big thing in their culture. I wondered why it bothered them so much about the drugs, since so many of the soldiers and other men in the camp were addicted to opium and heroin themselves.

During the first few weeks they were more private about the rapes, taking the girls out through the cement hall to the other side of the fence, but they eventually caught on to our camaraderie and of sticking together for moral support, so one of us wouldn't do something really stupid. Then about the fifth week they started raping us in front of the entire camp in order to shame us, so we wouldn't look each other in the eye, let alone talk to one another, out of shame and embarrassment. Not that we could talk all that much anyway. But body language told us a lot and we could sense the other person's feelings, especially in situations such as these.

At the time, I couldn't understand the concept behind the public rapes, if that's what you'd call them, but after returning to America, I learned a lot more about psychological warfare and how condemning the uses are.

Especially when you're forced to watch, like it's a movie premier, while the soldiers do horrible things to someone, all the while laughing. One look at anyone in the camp while this was happening would only elicit a look of pity, which made you feel even more worthless than you already did. Pretty soon it got to the point where no one would even glance at anyone else . . . we all felt ashamed, dirty, and totally broken by these bastards. What future did we have now?

140

The public rapes were so humiliating I can scarcely convey my feelings. But I will try. I can't say that the rapes were the most horrific things to ever happen to me. They were a far cry from enjoyment, for sure, but you have to understand the mentality of most of the people in the camp. Most were very strong willed people, which you have to be when you live in a country such as Iran, where you aren't allowed to ever show your true self due to the Islamic government restraints.

Especially on females. To live in Iran as a female means being very strong, very reserved, and very shy, and never showing your true emotions. The only reward I saw women get was to be able to prove to the men that the oppression they are forced live under does not effect them. The women of Iran are some of the strongest and most stubborn women I've ever met. They not only have to behave this way to survive, but must raise their daughters to the best of their ability in a society where women are second class citizens, and the only respect they receive is from their children. So, being a mother and a woman in Iran not only takes courage, but a strong backbone to survive the humiliation of the oppression which accompanies this. Older women are very respected in Iran, and the older they are, the more respect they get, not only from other women, but from the men as well. If you think about it, the older they are, the more experiences they have survived.

In the camp, while the women were mocked and punished openly without any reservations, it was their pride and their will to not succumb to the oppressors which was kept restrained. They didn't allow the soldiers to see their fear or indignation. This called for an especially strong front, which meant no show of tears, no emotions, and definitely no acts of surrendering. Although in truth, the whole camp experience was one massive surrender since no one had a choice in the matter. Not only did these women have to experience the rapes that were taken out in anger against them, and their ties to The Big Satan (USA), some were forced to endure this in front of their family members.

I had no family at the camp, only the acquaintances I'd made while there, but Faresh did. She had her brother and parents who were forced to witness her being hauled away to be raped, or they were forced to watch her being beaten, or any other actions taken against her. They had no choice, they were all there together.

In my eyes, these public rapes must have been more painful for Faresh to endure. Not only the physical pain that was inflicted on her, but knowing her parents had to witness it as well. In the end, the pain her parents went through while watching her endure this humiliation turned out to benefit her. More on this later.

The soldiers must have noticed the subtle support the women showed for each other whenever they brought one back from her rape sessions. In all actuality, we always anxiously awaited the person's return, since we were unsure if the person they took would ever return at all. So, in a way, when the girl was brought back, we were happy that she wasn't killed, yet, at the same time sad that she had to return to suffer more pain.

Anyway, the soldiers must have caught on to our silent support of one another and rather than risk any type of revolt, they decided to start doing the rapes publicly. I learned after I got back home and did some research, that it was to enforce a feeling of total shame on us to the point where we couldn't look at each other. Thus reducing our support system. It worked.

Faresh was the first to be publicly raped, probably due to her family being in the camp with her. They dragged her up in front of the camp and stated in a loud voice that this is what happens to people who associate with American whores, or who desire to be like American whores. They liked to refer to all American women as whores. I still believe this is due to their underlying jealousy, since whenever I had contact with an Iranian, outside of this camp, they were all respectful. Yet here in this camp, they couldn't degrade Americans enough.

Faresh was thrown on the ground and told to remove her pants, which she did mechanically from all the previous rapes. She did this while the other soldiers taunted her with words and phrases, such as, "You like to be fucked, don't you?" And, "You are like the American whore who likes to fuck all the time."

Faresh kept her face blank, never once looking towards any of the people in the camp. The first soldier who took her was far from gentle, but didn't seem to slap her as much as the second soldier did. When the third soldier got to her, he made her position herself on her stomach and face the camp of people, so everyone could see her.

This brought her to tears, along with a screaming fit. She called them all dirty bastards. Which brought another soldier up to smack her in the face with the butt of his gun, while the other soldier was still busy raping her.

She kept screaming, "Hit me! Hit me again, you bastard!"

I knew at that moment exactly how she felt. I had been there myself. When I wanted them to hit me so much they'd lose control and hit me once too often so that death settled in, then all my pain and humiliation would disappear. But of course, this never happened.

When they were through, they asked her if she'd had enough? She didn't reply, only stared blankly at the ground. They asked her again. Still no reply. When they asked her once more, she screamed, "No, I want more! I want to be like the American whores. Give me more," or words to that effect. They pushed her down and told her to crawl back to her place in camp.

It seemed that these soldiers had no qualms about exposing themselves in front of the whole camp or each other. It was like they had no self-respect at all. Their purpose was to humiliate all of us. And this they achieved.

When she returned, another soldier was right behind her to put the handcuffs back on. I was glad to see him coming, since this meant they wouldn't take me today. Wrong!

The soldier was coming to get me. He took my arm and shoved me ahead of him, and said, "Your turn, American whore!"

I escaped in my mind, like I usually did during the daily rapes. I detached myself from the situation while my body reacted like it was on automatic pilot. I don't recall when or how I got so good at this defense mechanism, but it sure came in handy, and still does today, even when I try to fight it.

When I got up in front of the camp, they removed my scarf. Yes, the women were still required to wear scarves to cover their hair while in camp. Even though I had only been left with my sports bra and jeans from my previous sessions with the Captain and his rifle barrel, I was still required to wear a scarf. I later found out the rifle barrel had ruptured my uterus and gone into my abdominal cavity.

Can you believe what a hypocritical religion these ass-holes depicted Islam to be? They shouted to the camp that this was the true face of Satan, meaning America. And that this was the true face of an

143

American whore. One who liked to be fucked and take money from men for fucking.

I don't know where they got their ideas, but most have been universally ingrained from long term lectures by their religious leaders.

At this point I can only explain my mind-set. I had been raped so many times by then that I no longer took it personally, nor could I take it as personal hurt, either. It was like going through a daily chore you're forced to do against your wishes. There was no more physical pain, since my mind was no longer focused on the act, but rather on things that had happened in my past which were unpleasant, but by no means to this degree. I had already fixed it into my daily behavior, not to let them see me suffer, so crying wasn't an option any longer.

Now this new idea of theirs, to publicly humiliate us, was right there in the front of my mind, and I had already been trying to come up with how I was going to react when it first happened to Faresh. It was survival in its most heinous form, as I'm sure it was for the others, too. And no one should judge us for how we reacted or chose not to react to these circumstances, until they've been in the same situation. I kind of had a feeling what they were up to with this, but was not clearly thinking due to malnutrition, and the hope that with each new atrocious experience, it would wrap-up this horrific epoch in my life.

When I was positioned in front of the camp, I too could not look at the people, but rather just stared at the soldiers, like I normally did, to irritate them. But more to show them I wasn't terrified enough to look away. I couldn't let them see fear, although it existed all right, and the detaching of my mind seemed to work well. I would actually become so involved with my thoughts of the past, that I was unsure of what stage we were in of the rape and humiliation scene. I don't remember everything that happened in front of the camp that day, but I do remember returning to Faresh afterward and being very quiet and subdued. I had blood seeping from my eye and mouth, and probably my nose as well from being slapped and punched during the rape. Because of my detachment during these times I can't recall everything. However, their tactic worked. I sure didn't want to look at anyone in the camp.

Since I couldn't recall all the details of what happened, I wasn't sure I wanted to see the other prisoner's reactions. It was sort of like an alcoholic who thinks his secret drinking has been well hidden, but was now exposed for everyone to see. Although the rapes happened, and all the girls knew it happened, as well as the men, it took on a deeper level of shame when it happened right there in front of everyone else. The soldiers had accomplished their goal.

We not only didn't look at each other now, I also felt a new level of discomfort with Faresh. Not that I was ever comfortable there, mind you, but a certain awkwardness was now present which I couldn't define, nor make disappear.

I felt like I had been so abused and used that no man would ever want me again. Not to mention even if he did, the minute we became intimate, he would realize I was just used merchandise and change his mind – that is, if I ever allowed for any sex to happen again. At this point, in the camp when all this happened, I never thought I would even speak to another human again out of fear and embarrassment, and never wanted to trust anyone again, let alone a man.

CHAPTER 16

Death

I won't lie, I wished for death and prayed for death many times. But this was due to my own selfishness of not wanting to endure any more pain. It would have been a whole lot easier to just lie down and go to sleep and never wake up, rather than face any unknown fate and more unknown torture.

The public and also private rapes continued almost daily, and so did the soldiers giving us heroin injections into our gums, involuntarily, so as to not cause such chaos when they came to get one of us.

But the heroin eventually was overused by one stupid soldier on Nasreen, and she ended up dying of an overdose. I think they overdosed the drug on her to calm her down as she tended to cry a lot more than the rest of us women. Also, she was quite young, being only around seventeen or so. I felt at peace for her to actually see her sleeping after having a heroin injection, as this seemed to calm her down more. I know she always had a look of hopelessness and desperation on her young face. Faresh and I tried to hide our fear, to not let the soldiers see how afraid and terrorized we were, but Nasreen did not. No matter how much the soldiers yelled at her or made threats, she still cried. It was as if she knew she had nothing to lose, so let it all out.

After her last heroin injection I think she knew she was going to die. She was chained next to me, not with me, but rather next to me. She slipped me a silver ring she had on, in passing, and said I would always be her friend. She died soon after.

The soldiers took her away and burned her body like a pig at a roast.

This, I believe, was for the purpose of not having a body around for people to ask questions about, or else to further intimidate us. Whatever sick reasoning they had, they burned her body, then cut off chunks of her flesh for us all to eat a piece.

They must have considered this an act of good will or something, since they had not fed us in approximately two weeks, nor did they ever feed us very much while we were there, other than leftover scraps from their own meals. And these were fought over by the prisoners who could grab them first. If you were not close to a guard after he finished his meal, you got left out, unless he threw them your way.

I actually felt kind of jealous of Nasreen when she died. When I accepted her ring, I never took it off until I returned to America. It was only silver, so I knew it wouldn't be taken from me, like my engagement ring had. That was made with sapphire and diamonds and was a very expensive piece of jewelry. I knew I would never see it again. The poetic justice concerning my ring was that one week prior to being seized and taken to this camp, I had lost the original sapphire out of the ring, so Mohammad had it replaced with a teardrop sapphire that was of less value.

A few hours after Nasreen died, I had already come to the conclusion that this had to be the best thing for her, and now she was in no more pain and could not be tortured any more. When I smelled the smoke and the strange odor coming from what looked like a pig on a big skewer the soldiers were roasting, there were no emotions. Even after overhearing the soldiers say it was Nasreen, no tears came. What good would it do? I rationalized. She was gone from her body now, and would never have to be humiliated, or degraded again. I wanted to be where she was, so badly, that jealousy was the only emotion I could muster at the time. I don't mean I wanted to be roasted, but dead like she was. The sad thing is that she had no family in the camp, she was alone. Therefore, her family may not ever know what happened to her, or how she died. As far as they are concerned, she disappeared off the face of the earth. Unless someone from the camp knew how to contact her family after they themselves survived. I didn't know anything about her family or how to contact them.

I can't stress enough how detached I still feel today from most of my emotions. I know what I should feel, but the only thing I feel is guilt for not feeling those emotions I'm <u>supposed</u> to be feeling. I wonder at times if I will ever be able to feel appropriately again. I question my own sanity at times. Why am I like this? Why can't I cry when I should? Why can't I feel pain for another human being when I should? It's all enough to drive me crazy at times.

I'm told it's due to getting so good at detaching while in the camp in order to survive the events and the tortures. I still cannot find the right answers to soothe those burning questions in my mind, but this is one reason for relating my story, in hopes that another human being will never have to endure this type of environment again.

* * *

Anyway, the soldier's act of good will was to make each one of us eat a piece of Nasreen's cooked flesh.

I could not do it, so I tucked it away in the side of my mouth until they'd passed by, then I spit it out. I think somebody else must have grabbed it and eaten it afterward, since it wasn't there later, after awakening from a short nap of about fifteen minutes. Which sleeping that long at one time was a miracle to me, since I hadn't slept much since arriving there. Well, being knocked unconscious does not technically count as sleep, does it?

* * *

A bit more about what we ate. We ate whatever crawled our way, literally. Be it insect, or rodent. We often ate these bugs that resembled grasshoppers. One Pakistani lady told me not to eat them when they were dead because they released a poison from their legs when dead. I don't know if this was true, but I ate them alive anyway. We ate ants, flies, field mice, or whatever type of rodent they were. We were not allowed to have fires, therefore anything we caught had to be eaten raw. I never personally killed a mouse, but a man chained down a bit from us caught one. It may have been another type of rodent, as it seemed a bit larger than just a field mouse. He tore its head off with his hands by holding it down on the ground with his foot. He then tore off it's limbs and passed them to the women. It wasn't the best, but when you're starving to death, you'll try things you never thought you might try. I figured if coyotes or other predators ate them whole, then they must be digestible. I peeled the fur down its leg, trying to detach it from the meat. I ate the uncooked meat and muscle from the small bones. It was still warm and somewhat stringy. It had a slight aftertaste that was a bit like charcoal. That's the only way I can describe it.

I got used to eating the grasshoppers. I could feel them moving inside my mouth, since I ate them alive. Even after I bit into them, I could still feel them moving sometimes. I got used to that first spray of juice that usually came with the first bite. But I'd hold my nose and swallow it after chewing it a bit more. Afterward, I'd lick sweat off my arms (which tasted salty) and anywhere else I could, to get the bitter taste out of my mouth. Though I got to where I craved the somewhat sweet aftertaste.

Ants were nothing to eat after that. We also would let mosquitoes bite us a few times, then eat them. One man told us we could get nourishment from our own blood this way. Again, I don't know if this is true, but I ate them anyway.

Just to taunt us, the guards would sometimes eat in front of us, but they usually stayed away during meals, since we were treated like animals and the smell in camp was awful. Of course we hadn't been able to wash in all the time during our captivity. Then add to this the smell of urine and feces from all the prisoners. The camp was not a pretty sight. Therefore, they usually preferred to eat their meals away from us. Then they would throw us their few scraps when they were finished.

The guards only came around when they wanted something, like to rape one of the women, or to torture us.

There were other horrific incidences.

One was when the soldiers took a son (he was about eighteen to twenty years old) from his parents. The soldiers unchained him and put a blindfold on him. I thought they were taking him out to question him. His father began to scream and beg for them to take him instead of his boy. The mother was weeping very loudly also. They then took the whole family, the mother, father, and the son. I was confused and didn't know what was going on. After about five minutes, we heard several gun shots. Not just one or two, but a massive amount of gun fire. Not like machine gun fire, but a lot of individual rifle shots.

150

I thought, my God, they've killed the whole family! I'd pretty much succumbed to the feeling that this was how we were all going to be killed. After about five more minutes passed, the soldiers returned with the parents, but without the son. I was in shock. We knew then what the outcome was. The bastards had executed the son right in front of his parents!

How cruel and unjust and uncalled for. The father had a very grim look on his face, like he was determined not to cry, but the mother had her head down with her hands over her face. I couldn't understand how they resisted the urge to not lie down and scream for the soldiers to shoot them too, and not care what else happened to them. These people had just witnessed the most horrific scene of their lives and survived it.

If anyone killed my son in front of me like that, I was sure I wouldn't want to live any longer either. Yet these people didn't react like that. I couldn't understand it. I felt so horrible for them and wanted to go to them and comfort them, but I couldn't. I had no clue how to let them know that I cared about their tragedy, but they refused to look at anyone. I think they may have felt guilt that their outburst might have caused their son's execution.

It was then I finally realized that some people are like sheep. They become so mesmerized in pleasing their superiors, no matter if it's right or wrong. They brainwash themselves into believing what they are doing is right. This is why there are so many martyrs in Islamic countries. They are brainwashed from birth to believe the ultimate sacrifice and most prestigious thing they can do in their life is to die for Allah's sake.

Therefore, when they decide to strap bombs on themselves, or die in other suicidal fashions that involve killing masses of people who do not believe in Allah or the laws of Islam, it is all justified to them from birth. In a way, I admire this dedication, though I don't agree with it, and think it is horrible how they try to take innocent lives. This is still murder. But purely from the perspective of their dedication, there are few other religions that would require this. I don't think there are many Christians or other religious groups which have this many dedicated people in their congregations. Now before you criticize my reasoning, remember, I'm just looking at it from the dedication standpoint. To be willing to die for your God.

Now in retrospect, here I would like to add that the parents might have at first reacted as they did with the father screaming due to the hideous consequences their son faced, but after seeing him die, they probably rationalized that he was now an honorary member in Allah's heaven due to his death. I don't know if this is true, but it's the only rationalization that fits with them acting so calm upon their return. Unless the son was actually released and the rifle shots were for the benefit of the rest of us prisoners. But the parents didn't act like this was case. I don't think they were that good of actors.

We are the only species I know of who are aware of our own mortality. I felt truly bad for these parents who endured the death of their son. I also felt bad the first time and second time that Faresh was taken to be raped. I felt terrible about Nasreen dying at the hands of an idiot who injected her with too much heroin.

But along with every tragedy came a relief in knowing I had somehow survived it.

The parents of the boy were taken about a week later. I don't know what became of them.

* * *

We used to hear choppers fly overhead and hoped that one of them was a rescue team. I used to daydream about my Uncle flying in, since he'd been a chopper pilot in Vietnam, but this was to no avail. The choppers were never our rescuers.

Although, once one landed, only to deliver more heroin to the soldiers.

Just a note here: There seemed to be a lot of opium and heroin use in Iran, Iraq, Turkey, Afghanistan, and other surrounding countries.

It was cheap if you bought it with American dollars. Something like $3.00 for a day's habit. Which is about as cheap as a pack of cigarettes. This translates into 2,400 to 4,800 Tomans, which is their currency over there. The exchange rate at the time was $1 American = 800 Tomans, or 8000 Rials.

I believe this was how my husband became so addicted to it, due to it being so cheap and readily available, despite it being against the law, as well as against the Muslim religion as well. I think this was one of the reasons why Bin Ladin was rumored to have made the comments he did.

Despite all the derogatory things the soldiers said about Americans and how our youth are involved with so many drugs, there seems to be an almost universal addiction among the men there. I think it's their only escape from the rigors of government and religious control over their lives.

CHAPTER 17

Russian Roulette

W<!-- -->e were eventually transferred to a third camp. This one looked the same as the others. This trip took us almost all day to arrive at our destination, so where we were was anybody's guess. The moves involved all the same events as before. That is, being blindfolded, pushed into the back of a truck, not being allowed to talk to anyone. However, the handcuffs and chains remained in the camp, I'm sure for the next group of poor victims. But they always had other chains and cuffs which were used upon arriving at our new destination.

The faces of the guards did change somewhat, though there were still a few of the same ones, but for the most part, we had many new guards with which to endure more torture under.

I remember the first time they transferred us. One of the girls thought they were going to take us back and drop us off where they'd picked us up, such as the bus station or airport, or worse, home. But I understood their language, probably better than she did, and knew all too well where we were headed. But I allowed her to cling to her fantasy for the time being. We all needed an escape from reality at times in order to endure the forthcoming hell that had been promised to us all.

By the third move there were only approximately eighteen to twenty people still left in the camp. Some had been taken from the camp from time to time, never to be heard from again. We didn't know if they were set free, or taken out somewhere and shot. We had no idea what happened to them. Or some, like Nasreen and the boy who was executed in front of his family, died in the camp. I worried we might eventually all be killed since I had seen it happen with the boy whose parents were forced to watch. I was certain things were about to change with the new move. However, besides Nasreen and the boy, I don't think anyone else perished that we knew for <u>sure</u>, at the hands of the soldiers. But again, this is just a guess.

There were many moments unaccounted for, like when they came to get me and take me out for their daily dose of fun (rapes and torture), and upon returning the people there could never really divulge any events which happened during my absence, unless they were willing to face some type of physical punishment for it. We were all just biding our time, hoping for the best, but too often expecting the worst.

The nights started getting colder, especially now that we were at our third transfer. This camp had the same basic set up as the last two. We saw only mountains around us, but <u>which</u> mountains I had no idea. I couldn't even be sure I was in Iran any longer, due to the long travel time involved with the transfer. We could have crossed over any border which might be nearby. We weren't too far from Afghanistan.

As a political note here, I'd like to add that everyone in Iran who was able to speak to each other freely, would always talk of how Saddam and Osama Bin Laden had bomb shelters in the Damavad Mountains in Tehran. People also claimed they rode around together in a brown Mercedes with an Afghani flag on the back and an Iraqi flag on the front of the car. This didn't sound too out of the ordinary for me. I'd also heard a rumor that if America bombed Afghanistan in retaliation, that Bin Ladin would lower the heroin prices so ridiculously low that almost anyone could afford it. I don't know how these go hand in hand, but I do think he carried out his last threat for whatever reason. I say this in jest with a hardened heart, since the soldiers were injecting us with heroin. I can't figure out what his reasoning was behind the drug comment, unless he is addicted also. After all, taking drugs is against Muslim laws, so why he thought lowering the prices was a solution to anything, I can't say. I just know that it seems to be in common use among most of the men in Iran. Although we have a drug problem in the USA, it is nothing compared to what goes on behind closed doors in Iran.

Around mid October, we heard rumors that a Blackhawk helicopter had flown in, in order to view the area to verify rumors that Americans were being held in these camps. I almost became excited. ALMOST. If you go back and read the news archives, I'm sure you will also read that a Blackhawk helicopter crashed around mid October. Anyway, wherever we were at the time, the news of this crash was the general excitement amongst the soldiers that week. They felt they had won! At least this particular battle, anyway.

* * *

As I said, around the end of October, due to people being sporadically removed from the camps, either by freedom, or death, there only remained about twenty people or less. I couldn't give you an exact count due to my state of mind from starvation and the heroin injections.

Faresh and her family, and I were amongst those, but we were also dying of starvation.

I figured if we weren't killed in some other way the rest of us were doomed to start dying soon of malnutrition. I think I had probably lost close to sixty or seventy pounds. My spine ached so badly from lack of calcium and other vitamins that it was becoming difficult to walk. I had always wanted to be skinny, but not to the point of looking like an Ethiopian famine victim. But then again, you think of strange things when you have a lot of time on your hands.

I did an ant study here as well, since there were many ant hills in the camp with us. I used to marvel at their teamwork. If only we could all get a plan going as well as those ants did, maybe we could get the hell out of there. When I wasn't studying the ants, I ate them.

Faresh had built up a small mound of dirt which she would lie on at night because her back hurt so much. It acted like a back support for her when she'd sleep. It was sort of her way of personalizing our bit of space there at the camp. That small mound of dirt was one of the things I looked forward to seeing after I was brought back from our daily rapes by the soldiers. It became something familiar to me that I could relate to after being tortured. Like coming home to familiar surroundings after a rough day away. I know it sounds weird, but you cling to small things like that when you are being emotionally and physically devastated on a daily basis.

* * *

About this time the soldiers tried out a new game to torture us.

Russian Roulette. There was an unidentified man who was supposedly new and coming into the camp. We never saw his face since it was covered with a black hood. When they gave him a gun for the first time and made him pull the trigger, nothing happened. The second time he pulled the trigger the gun went off. He fell down and we looked away. I wasn't close enough to see any blood, but I thought there would be a much bigger hole in the black hood he was wearing if a bullet had passed through it. Who knows if he was someone they in fact killed, or if he was just acting in order to scare us out of any thoughts of escaping or causing chaos.

* * *

As I've said before, the soldiers didn't particularly care for Faresh and I, and one day after not having any injections for a few days, they approached us and gave us each some heroin. I was ready to pass out from pure exhaustion and starvation, coupled with the action of the drug, when I was pulled to my feet, along with Faresh, by two soldiers who said it was our day to die.

I really didn't care any more at this point. I figured if I had to die, then I should thank them for allowing me to go pain free.

They shoved us onto the ground up in front of the camp, which everyone knew as the podium. This was where they humiliated people, conducted the public rapes, where they barked their orders, and where they supposedly killed the person no one knew. They slipped a couple of black hoods over our faces. The hoods felt more like a silky cotton, but were totally blinding. I couldn't see any daylight through it.

They told us they were going to play a favorite game of Americans in the movies, called Russian Roulette. However, in my drug induced state, I thought he had said Roseanna Arquette, and while I knew her name as an actress, I couldn't associate her with any death games. I finally caught on when I felt a gun pressed against my head, a little above my temple. Before I knew it, I heard a click. No warning, no chance to get the heart rate going, just a click, then Faresh screaming.

I heard her fall over next to me and figured maybe her gun had a silencer on it since I didn't hear it go off and thought they'd shot her somewhere. The guards started to laugh hysterically and called us crazy bitches and whores. God, how I wanted those bastards to die in the worst possible way.

They then said, to the effect, "Let the bitch whores shoot themselves."

I supposed they were going to give us the guns in order to make it look like a suicide. So when they handed us the guns, I spoke to Faresh in English, since most of the soldiers couldn't understand much English, let alone metaphors. I said, "You take 9 o'clock, and I will take 2 o'clock," meaning that if we were going to die, then we should take out a couple of these jerks with us.

Faresh understood, or at least put two and two together, but after I said it, the guard hit me in the face and spoke to me in Farsi, telling me to shut up and pull the trigger.

I knelt on the ground with my heart beating louder than my breathing. All the while I was trying to listen for the guard's breathing so I could generalize his location and try to shoot him when I pulled the trigger. When I did, and I will never know how close I came with my aim, the gun only clicked. I pulled the trigger again and again.

Nothing. I was preparing myself to die. Actually, welcoming the chance by this point. Then I held the gun to my own head and hoped there was at least one bullet in it, because I wasn't ready to face another beating, especially the kind I knew we were sure to get. Well there wasn't one, and the sound of the hollow empty clicking of the chamber nauseated me to the point of dry heaves. I knew we were in for it.

After this they yanked our hoods off and we were beaten pretty severely in the face and head. This is where the second boot indentation in my skull came from. Not to mention a fractured jaw, and half of my teeth being kicked out, or broken off. Faresh got the same treatment, if not worse.

Then we were taken one by one outside the camp where we were hit with whips, hands, belts, and anything else within striking distance. I didn't even try to explain or answer questions, not that I understood much what was being said in my dazed state. Every few minutes a new soldier would come in and get briefed on what Faresh and I did.

They hung us by our wrists in one part of the camp where it was said they hanged prisoners. It looked sort of like a wooden base for a swing-set. However, it was high enough to allow us to dangle. Our wrists were tied with ropes that were then strung over the upper beam, then we were lifted off the ground and left to hang there. It felt like my shoulders were going to tear out from their sockets at any moment. The pain was horrendous. We hung like that for about an hour.

Now this might not sound like a long time to some, but let me tell you, <u>one minute</u> is <u>toooo</u> long in that position! We were beaten sporadically by any given soldier who walked by. I think one soldier wanted to spray us with some type of acid, but his commander told him, not to. Not yet.

When they returned us to what might be considered the general population of the camp, we were horribly bruised and our eyes so swollen it was hard to see. Faresh and I just sat there, not even looking at each other. I could barely think. I was in a sort of daze or stupor, almost like a trance, and nothing could stir me from it. I'm sure Faresh felt the same way. I don't know how we remained conscious after that beating. There was very little movement by us for the remainder of the day. Probably the only thing that helped dull the pain was the heroin injection they gave me not long before the beatings.

* * *

That night, I started to cry. I had no idea where the tears came from. It might have been that I had basically given up hope of ever leaving that place alive. Maybe I was finally venting all the grief, pain, and torture I'd suffered for all those weeks. We'd been held in the camps for at least six weeks by now, and I felt I was going to eventually die there, either by starvation, or at the hands of the soldiers.

Normally I tried to hold back any emotion in order to not give the guards the satisfaction of seeing me cry or that my spirit had been broken, but for some reason, I could not hold back the tears this time. I did try to recycle the tears, though. Eventually I fell into sort of a state of grogginess or stupefaction and dozed off.

I was convinced I must have suffered some type of permanent brain damage after what happened next.

I heard a voice in my ear, very distinct and clear, say, "<u>Lori, you are going home</u>."

I jerked around immediately to see who was mocking me.

It was a soft, soothing voice, but when I looked around to see who was speaking, no one was stirring in the camp. They either were asleep or else acting quite well. I figured I must have suffered brain damage from all the blows to my head, and was now hearing auditory hallucinations. When I couldn't see anyone near me besides Faresh, who was asleep, I settled back in.

I knew it wasn't Faresh's voice I'd heard, as the voice was male.

Then I felt the soft touch of a hand on my shoulder.

I again jerked around to see who was taunting me. No one was there.

I can tell you this, I'd never felt more serene or at peace than I did at that moment when I felt the soft touch on my shoulder. It was like being wrapped in a warm blanket and soothed by someone who loves you.

However, I took the meaning of the words in a totally different way than what they were apparently intended. I thought of "going home" to mean dying and going home to be with God. Which I had no qualms about then, nor did I argue with. I was ready to die. I'd taken all the beatings I could take.

I felt an uneasy calm the rest of the night.

It wasn't until later that I interpreted this voice as a message from God.

CHAPTER 18

Escape

I can vividly recall the day the soldiers decided to play Russian Roulette with us and the severe beating we got. It had been approximately six weeks that we'd been in these God forsaken camps (now the third), and I was so sick of surviving day to day, that I truly wished for death. That is . . . until the man named Abbey gave us something to hope for.

The next night after I'd heard the voice in my ear and felt the soft touch on my shoulder, much to my surprise, Faresh's brother, Abbey (this is what they called him in Bahrain, to mean a man who is so giving), had somehow either paid off a guard, or bribed them, to allow me and Faresh to escape under the fence.

Abbey had been trying to get my attention all day, and at one time he and Faresh, who was still chained to me, were communicating via lip messages. But I didn't ask what they were talking about. After the soldiers were finished eating that night, and had started their routine of smoking opium, I noticed that the one guard who usually sat near us wasn't there. Whatever Abbey had promised the soldier, it must have been good, since I was sure he was in for major physical punishment when their superior found out. Abbey was telling us to hurry up and he actually had the key to our cuffs. He took our cuffs off us.

Faresh yanked me up, and said, "Let's go."

I said, "Go where?"

She then said, "Shh . . . just follow me."

Abbey was over by the fence and pushed the dirt away from the bottom, then held the fence up over the dirt mound it was entrenched in. No one else watched, they turned their heads away. They didn't want to witness this. Or they were just too sad that it wasn't them. This is when the guilt set in for me, but I figured if we could get back to some moral civilization then I could send help to save them too.

The fence was cut under the first few inches of dirt so that it still looked intact, until you shoved the easily removable dirt mounds away.

Due to my severe starvation, fitting under the small space and crawling out to freedom was, for once, not a problem for me. We frantically burrowed underneath the fence and all the while I kept asking Abbey if he was coming with us?

His reply was no, he had an obligation to stay with his ill parents.

Obligation to die, was more like it, I thought. I felt so sad for him, yet at the same time a sense of pride that such a noble man had helped us reach our freedom. So, Abbey stayed behind with his parents since they were both too sick to make the journey. I was all too unaware of what might lay ahead for us.

After we were allowed out from under the fence, we were met by two men. They didn't speak either English or Farsi, but could only say, "Shalom," which means peace. THANK GOD, I thought, because at first I was certain these two men were there to take us back and execute us.

You learned not to trust anyone by then. But – and, yes, I know this sounds incredulous, it was for me as well – these two men had two llamas waiting for us to ride, while they led them. I was told later that they were probably not llamas but some type of small one humped camel which the hump could have been concealed by the blankets that were on them. I was also told that the reasoning behind me thinking this was probably due to my severe malnutrition, and frame of mind at the time."

When they quickly uttered the word "Shalom," we calmed down a little, but I was still taken aback by our mode of transportation. I thought to myself, camels, yes, horses, yes, but llamas? I had no idea there were llamas in Iran, let alone that you could ride them. But apparently you can if you don't weigh too much. There were rugs, similar to a horse's blanket piled on the llamas' backs and necks, and covering their eyes somewhat. Probably to protect their eyes from blowing sand, or maybe to keep the animals quiet.

I crawled up on the beast with the aide of the man who was leading it, and adjusted myself for what would be a long ride back to civilization. But where were they going to take us, I wondered?

About two hours into the llama ride, the men stopped. I didn't speak the men's language and wondered if we were going to be shot and dumped out there in the middle of nowhere. The men motioned with their hands for us to get down off the llamas. I thought, this was it. They were going to abandon us and make us find our own way home by ourselves. Or worse, that they were going to kill us.

Instead they dug into some dirt that looked like it had been recently churned up and thrown back over whatever was underneath it. There was a bag buried next to a tree.

It turned out to contain fresh fruit, figs, bananas, dried meat, and water. They handed us water bottles and some dried meat.

God, that was heaven sent . . . the salty meat made the water taste that much better, although the water alone was almost too good to be true. Even though it was warm, it still tasted wonderful.

They also had two black chadors for us to wear. I didn't want to don the chador right away, since I was struggling to stay on the llama, and figured it would be hard to keep the chador wrapped around me and hold on to it, besides trying to hold onto the llama. For some reason they seldom put snaps or buttons on the chadors to help keep them on. The women are expected to hold them in place with their hands. But Faresh caught some of their conversation and said that if we passed any other travelers on the road, we would appear as normal wives out with their husbands. I objected to that, and asked what was normal about two women out in the middle of nowhere on LLAMAS? Faresh started to giggle, and so did I, to the point we almost fell off these creatures.

The llamas doubled as watch dogs too. Any noise, even if it was too low or high pitched for us to hear, the llamas would let out a sort of donkey type bray. It scared the shite out of me the first time it happened. I was dozing off on the ride and had my head resting against the back of the llama's neck, which was covered by the rug. I heard that noise and my first thought was of a prison warden sounding alarms for two escaped convicts. It's funny now in retrospect, but it wasn't then.

I drank so much of the wonderful fresh water that I got severe cramps and had to stop for a while. This is when the llama tried to bite me . . . that smelly, hairy animal with the bad attitude, yet he remained beautiful to me, tried to bite me on the shoulder. I was standing bent over, trying to get the cramps to subside when I heard one of the men come up behind me and start yelling while he hit the llama on the nose. It bleated out in pain. Sort of sounded like a sheep. Anyway, the man could not tell me what happened, but I inferred it by the way he made a face of gnashing teeth. Boy was I lucky . . . to make it all this way, then nearly be eaten by a llama. The mere idea of it sent me into a hysterical laughing fit.

Only Faresh could see the humor in it though, since the men didn't understand our language. I crawled back up on my llama, my beautiful ticket home, to continue the ride. Because we were traveling through the mountains, I could now understand why they had the llamas. The creatures are originally from South America and are used as pack animals in the high Andes Mountains and are fairly sure footed over rough terrain.

I did go through some heroin withdrawals while on the way. I had back pain, hot and cold chills, along with aches and pains in my hips and other stuff.

The men had brought dried fruits and a lot of water, but they were stored at unusual spots along the journey back. This path must have been used before, for them to have all these hiding places out in the middle of nowhere, the way the food was cached.

I was also given some clothes and shoes, since all I was wearing was a sports bra and jeans. My shoes had been taken when I had my feet beaten by the leather straps and my cuts had gotten infected. Later I did discover that the montou I'd been given had buttons to hold it closed, so it was not intolerable during the llama ride.

That first night on the llamas was one of pure exhilaration for me to be away from that camp. Yet at the same time I was afraid it would all come to an end at any moment and they would find us and shoot us out there in the mountains, where no one would find us but the vultures. My emotions were so much on edge that I felt like just hopping off the llama and running as fast and as far as I could, even though I had no clue as to where we were or where I might run to.

We traveled for about two and a half days over the mountains back to the outskirts of Shiraz. We only took short breaks for food and water and to rest the llamas. The men took short naps while we rested, but we didn't spend a lot of time in one spot. I napped often while riding on the llama, leaning my head against its neck.

We came up a hill or ridge and when I looked over it, I could see

Ghastrodasht. This was a main road that went through the center of Shiraz. I gleefully ran down the large embankment to the very outskirts of Ghastrodasht, and when I mean the outer skirts of this famous road in Shiraz, I mean way out, since I had never seen this part of Ghastrodasht during my whole stay in Shiraz.

The llama ride stopped there, but it didn't matter. I felt somewhat at home, yet somewhat scared to death. Faresh informed me that her llama was going in a different direction. She pointed out where I should go.

She hugged me, and I asked why she wasn't going with me to Immigration. She said she couldn't divulge the reasons why, she only said it wouldn't be safe for her and that she was going on farther. I didn't ask where, but I did have a sense of loss, like when you know something big is about to change your whole life, but you're unsure of what. Sort of like when your best friend moves away and you have a feeling of loss, that you'll never see them again. We hugged and said goodbye, and that was it. I figured she was going to get more help in order to rescue her brother and parents from the camp.

Faresh had told me about Ostandary and what they were supposed to do for foreigners in trouble. Then she and the two men left. So, when we got to the edge of the city, Faresh went one way and I another.

I rushed down the hill to the road. I knew I was filthy. Even the chador I wore smelled like llama, besides not having washed for six weeks. But I also knew that there were still taxis in Shiraz that you didn't have to pay for until you got to where you were going. I'm guessing it was early morning when I arrived at that heavenly view atop the hill.

It wasn't quite light out, but it wasn't completely dark, either. Sort of an early morning gray. After I ran down the hill, I stopped and waited for one of those Peykan cars to stop and offer me a ride.

About five minutes passed and sure enough, there was a taxi. I told him to take me to Ostandary.

Ostandary is supposed to be a place where foreigners go if they run into trouble while in Iran. This organization was set up to help those who were in this strange land and have run into a crisis of one form or another.

Anyway, I immediately went to Ostandary which was supposed

to be a haven for foreigners in need of aid. As I said, it was <u>supposed</u> to be!

When I first walked in, I saw a mural painted above the doorway that stated, "If you had something taken from you in Iran (if you were robbed), then it is Iran's responsibility to pay you back the entire worth of the items taken." I thought to myself, what kind of price tag would accompany the loss of dignity, loss of independence, and on the whole, loss of self? I quickly concluded there would be no way they could ever repay me for what I'd endured at the hands of their fanatic natives.

They brought up a guy who spoke English rather well, and in no way looked Persian. He had blond curly hair and was in charge of assisting those who spoke English. I truly don't recall his name, so I will refer to him as "John," as in John Doe. John asked me what had happened and where my passport was? I replied that my husband and I were at the Shiraz bus terminal and I fell asleep and when I awoke he was gone and so were all the suitcases we had lugged there.

I couldn't tell anyone in Iran what <u>really</u> happened, since I didn't know if the government was involved or not. Although, I had a strong gut instinct that they were. I was afraid they would arrest me again and take me back to that camp.

John processed the false information I gave him and asked me if I had anything of worth, like money, rings, etc. I replied no, adding mentally, not even my self-worth, but I didn't say this out loud.

He showed me to a dormitory style room with three beds in it, then had a coworker bring me some fresh fruit; grapes, kiwi, and mangoes. He told me he would see what he could do for me. In the meantime, he told me to eat something, and the TV room was down the hall to the left. I shuffled toward the TV room, which was filled with Persians, or partly Persian boys, watching a soccer game.

They briefly looked up when I walked in. But since there were no scornful looks, or someone telling me to leave, I sat there for about an hour watching soccer.

John eventually came rushing into the TV room and exclaimed, "There you are! We thought you had left us." No such luck there. He then began to ask me how long I had lived in Iran, and did I give up my American passport, or for that matter, did I denounce my American citizenship.

"NO!" I replied emphatically, along with telling him how they had taken my passport upon arrival in the country over four years ago. He told me that was normal. He then said there was very little they could do for me, other than the exceptional offer to take me to my husband's family's house. The one I had once called home. From there I could maybe find out where my husband might be. I did allow them to do this, figuring I might find out some answers.

Upon arriving at the Foroozandeh house, I felt such a great sadness and homesickness. Yet at the same time a terrible fear that cancelled out the homesickness. When John knocked on the door, Narges, Mohammad's other sister, answered the door. I asked her where Mohammad was?

I was told, "Burrow-gome-shaw," from his sister. You might remember that this is a Farsi saying which means, "Get lost or go away and don't come back."

I couldn't understand what had gone so terribly wrong. Narges and I had been close before I left. We had helped her out when her husband was experiencing a mid-life crisis and left her for a much younger woman. Why was she saying this? I didn't understand.

Ostandary returned me to their headquarters for the night, but John told me that in the morning I would be shuffled to Iran's Immigration Office, and the International Police could handle it from there. He had told me that without a passport there was no way to verify if I were telling the truth. I told him to take me to the Zabanamoozan Language Institute and the principal there, if not the students, could verify who I was.

The school's secretary was Ms. Haghighat, and she would surely recognize me.

John said he couldn't do that, but would tell the Immigration Office and they could. What kind of help was this? I wondered. I was an American, couldn't they see that? Couldn't they hear my proficient English, combined with my very American accent?

CHAPTER 19

Still Captive in Iran

I spent the night at Ostandary. They gave me a hygiene kit with a toothbrush, small tube of toothpaste, small soap and shampoo. Like the kinds you get in hotels. This is when I took my first shower in six weeks. It felt almost foreign to me. To be able to stay under warm running water for as long as I wanted was the only luxury I could ask for at that very moment. It felt wonderful to be clean. Then the time came to brush my teeth.

When I first started scrubbing away, something dropped out into the sink. It was a tooth. I was sick to my stomach. Then I could feel other bits of hard pieces in my mouth, too, but I assumed this was dirt. You might remember I used to rub dirt on my gums and teeth to discourage the guards from kissing me during the rapes.

However, it was not dirt. It was pieces of my teeth! I was mortified.

I had come to Iran with a beautiful smile full of good healthy teeth. I was known for my smile. I had never had any cavities until I became pregnant at eighteen, and my first dentist asked me who had done my braces. My proud reply was that I never had braces. To see my smile literally going down the drain at this point did a huge amount of damage to what little self-esteem I had left.

I finally opened my mouth and looked at my teeth closely in the mirror. Or what was left of them. There were so many missing and broken off that this became overwhelming to me and sent me on a crying jag that lasted almost half an hour. Most of my broken teeth were the result of being kicked in the head and jaw after the Russian Roulette incident. Some might have been the result of malnutrition.

While it felt good to be clean again, I still didn't feel clean inside, or mentally. Whether it was due to the rapes, or the massive acts of humiliation, my mind told me I would never really be clean again. And this type of dirtiness isn't so easy to get rid of . . . if one <u>ever</u>

gets rid of it. They had literally and metaphorically taken away my smile.

I had teeth missing in the front and the side, and many others were broken off so that I looked like the hideous vision I'd always held of a true trailer trash skank on the Jerry Springer show. It was that very day I started the fine art of keeping my smiles to a minimum and never laughing out loud, since this would expose my broken and missing teeth.

My face was still badly bruised and contorted out of shape and I could feel the indentations of the boots from the kicks to my skull. It felt like a baby's soft spot. I figured this would heal with time, but my teeth would not. They were gone for good.

After showering and dealing with the initial shock of my mouth's condition, I remember just sitting there in pure numbness. I couldn't think, I couldn't even think of anything to think about. So, I slowly started looking at my body. I hadn't really paid much attention to it when I was getting undressed to shower, since the call of the water overshadowed any other thoughts at the time.

I truly figured that once I could rid my physical body of the filth, my mental faculties might feel a bit more cleansed as well. It didn't happen, though. I just sat there, trying to understand why it was I should feel embarrassed of ever having to face another human being again, let alone people I knew and loved. Now that the possibility was so much closer to reality, after all, I was out of the camp now, the thought suddenly horrified me.

I felt ashamed. When the people at Ostandary first talked to me, I felt so unworthy of even talking back to them. I don't know why. I'm sure there are a lot of theories on why I felt this way then, and still do to this day. But at the time, it was perplexing for me to figure it out.

I sat on the bed, first examining my feet, and seeing the gashes that were still sore and open, and needed Band-Aids, but were much better than they had been. Then I started looking at my legs.

My God! Where were my legs? I had always been somewhat chunky, but to finally realize and see for the first time the effects of my weight loss was quite overwhelming. My legs were just bones with skin over them. My knees looked like huge knobs on top of thin sticks. I rushed to the bathroom mirror and removed my shirt, to see nothing but a skeleton with shoulders and arms.

I'd always hated my arms because they looked fat to me, but standing there looking at my new body was not doing my self-esteem that much good. It was then that all these questions came to me, along with my sense of sarcastic humor.

My first thought was why men would be attracted to those stick-thin models who swayed down the catwalks and runways. I thought my body must mimic many of them, and how utterly horrible it looked. I'd always wanted to be skinny, but this was ridiculous. I had no breasts, my stomach was so caved in I could only get a little pinch of skin. My butt was just a bunch of hanging skin, but the thought of applying for one of those modeling jobs hit me in a sarcastic moment. I then thought of how my mother would react when she saw me like this. I couldn't picture myself this thin even at birth.

I just kept staring at every little aspect of my new body, realizing it was me. I knew the jeans I'd been wearing in the camp had become quite baggy, but I had no idea I had gone down that many pant sizes. When I first arrived in Iran, I wore a size 12 to 14 pants. By the time I returned home, I fit into a 1 to 2 size pants. In case you are wondering, I had held my jeans up while in the camp with a small piece of fabric that I'd ran through some of the belt loops.

Don't even wonder about a bra size. I had no breasts to fill out a bra. They had shrunk to nearly nothing.

After the initial shock wore off, and realizing that my body and teeth were history, I tried to think about what I would say or do when I first saw my family. Nothing came to mind. Total nothingness existed in my mind right then, and I seemed to operate on autopilot.

When I actually laid back on the bed, it was the first soft bed I'd slept on in over six weeks. It felt wonderful on my sore back. I think I slept a bit fitfully as this too was almost foreign to me. Again I thought of my mom's tuna casserole and sitting at home with them. I longed to be home and hoped that this would be the first leg of that journey.

* * *

The next morning, John awakened me and told me that the Immigration Police were waiting for me at the entrance. I quickly got ready and hurried out to greet them. They began questioning me right from the beginning, no hello, no how are you, just "Where did you come from, where is your passport," blah, blah, blah. I didn't understand why they couldn't figure out where my passport was, since this country took it from any woman upon arrival into the country.

They quickly found out that I was married to an Iranian, thus making me an Iranian citizen. Which also meant abiding by Iranian law. This meant I could not exit the country until my husband signed a permission slip for me to leave. I was sure this was all one big set-up and begged John to let me remain at Ostandary while they looked for my passport. He assured me they would put me up in one of the nicest hotels in Shiraz, until my passport was found.

He was right about everything, except the word "nicest."

I was taken to a typical rundown hotel, but on the bright side, it was an upper class rundown hotel. The Anvari Hotel located on Anvari Street. The police told the man at the desk that I was not to leave the hotel, "for my own safety." Right, I thought. You just don't want your prisoner to escape.

Before the police left me at the hotel, they asked me if there was anything special I needed. For some reason I told them, "Hair Gel." I know this sounds utterly ridiculous, but in my mind it was the one thing I thought would make me feel normal again, in that I could style my hair. Something I used to do before I was taken captive, something I used to do while living in the USA.

Ostandary gave me over to the Immigration International Police, which none of them could speak much English, well broken at best. The Immigration Office put me in the Anvari Hotel where they told the man on duty, who seemed to stay on duty 24/7, to guard me the entire stay. He was named Mansooreh, pronounced Man-soo-ray. He greeted me warmly with a smile, and took me upstairs to what was to be my room.

I asked him for a cigarette and he said he would see what he could do. He told me to take a shower and just relax. He became somewhat attached to me and asked me what grade I was in. Ha, ha, ha, they really filled him in on the details.

I was put in a room with no TV, geesh, and no PHONE! I couldn't even contact anyone to let them know I was alive and where I was. On that note, he left and <u>locked</u> me in my room! I was mortified and angry and sure that I would never see my home (USA) again. What right did they have locking me into a room? What if there was a fire or something? I yelled Mansooreh's name and he quickly bounded up the stairs to see what it was I so desperately needed.

I asked him why I was being locked in a room like a prisoner? Had I done something wrong, or was I considered bad in some way?

He assured me that none of that applied to me, but "for my own safety" I had to stay in the hotel. If I were to leave without a passport or any other form of ID, that "Allah only knew" (which is the equivalent of saying, "God only knows.") who might pick me up and cause trouble for me. He said that until some form of ID surfaced I could not be flown back to America. So, there I sat, with the only break in my boredom coming with my one meal of rice a day, or if I was lucky, some cheese and bread for breakfast. I'd merely traded one type of prison for another.

Of course, I should have been grateful for the bit of food I was given. I didn't realize it at the time, but if I'd had much more than the bland rice it would have caused me stomach problems due to its shrunken state and I wouldn't have been able to digest it without getting sick. To have a small bowl of rice once a day was more than I'd had in the last six weeks while starving in that camp. However, this does not fatten you up very quickly. I was so used to going without food, that it was hard to eat more than a small amount at a time. My stomach had shrunken down to nearly nothing so it couldn't hold very much, and even eating a couple of spoonfuls of the rice made me feel full. Therefore, the small bowl of rice lasted me most of the day. Sometimes I got a Kabob with the rice, but it was still hard to eat much.

I had access to drinking water, but again, I was so used to going without and with my stomach so small, I seemed to fill up fast with small amounts.

There was nothing to read, nothing to do but sit and listen to the planes take off and land . . . and dream of being on one headed for home. I had no other person to interact with. I missed having Faresh at my side. The room was very small, though it had one window that I could look out of, but not much of a view. It had its own bathroom which you had to step up into. The shower was on the same level as the toilet, so when you showered, it flooded the bathroom. But it always eventually drained. The toilet was the typical Iranian toilet which was just a tile encased hole in the floor that you squat over. They had air-conditioning, but it didn't work very well.

I did finally make friends with Mansooreh, and the cleaning girls, named Nahid and Narges. And after about a week, Mansooreh eventually let me start accompanying him on his daily inspections of the hotel rooms. He was your typical Persian, kind to a fault, oblivious to details and not wanting to know too much about the atrocities happening right under his nose in his own country. He must have wondered about the bruises around my eyes and swollen lips, my thin appearance. But I didn't dare tell him the truth for fear I would be sent back to the camp. After all, I was still pretty much a prisoner in the hotel.

Eventually he let me go downstairs to the diner and the TV room, which were one and the same, depending when you chose to enter. He told me I could not leave the hotel, nor go near the exit door. I agreed. It was so nice to just get out of that room and to be able to see others, even if I wasn't allowed to talk to them. At least not yet.

Occasionally he had Mrs. Anvari, the hotel owner's wife, come and pick me up to stay with her for the day at their beautiful home. It was filled with expensive furniture and decor. She had two children, a boy and a girl. Mostly she had me go there while her husband had gone to Sweden with his parents on a trip. I'm sure she was trying to entertain me and keep me from feeling lonely. I know she must have known what happened to me, but she didn't ever want to talk about it. If I tried to tell her about being kidnaped and all the horrors that went on, she and her husband would dismiss my story like it was something preposterous and funny. They would change the subject quickly. They didn't want to know what happened within their own government.

I think part of the reason Mansooreh had Mrs. Anvari pick me up was that he was afraid I would starve to death there in the hotel and they would hold him responsible. He would sometimes yell at me to eat more and on occasion actually try to feed me! I have to admit, the quality of the food was good, but I just couldn't eat once my stomach felt full. Which only took a couple of spoonfuls of rice to fill. They could see how thin I was, I'm sure, even under my clothing.

176

I did eventually manipulate Mansooreh, the hotel manager, into allowing me one phone call to the USA, my mother's house. However, she still had the attitude that I was only calling to get drug money (which I didn't learn about until after I returned home), and again acted distant and guarded.

At the time I couldn't understand her attitude. I tried to tell her to get someone to fax a copy of my passport to the Immigration Office in Iran, so they would know who I was. All I could do was wait and hope she would follow through.

The first few days at the hotel when I was still locked in my room, I tried filling my days with counting the minutes, then crossing off each hour on the wall with a pencil I'd found under the bed. Then I got really energetic and started writing a letter home on the toilet paper wrapper. When it is reversed it is blank on the other side. The days were monotonous. I mean, no TV, no phone, no conversation, no reading material. Just like being in a prison. Not even ants to study. There was not much to look at from the window, so I couldn't even people watch.

Then eventually I was allowed to go down to the lobby with Mansooreh. The reason he started allowing me to go to the lobby was he thought that having an American sitting there would be good for business. They love Americans, yet are taught to hate those who don't believe the same as they do. It's a love/hate relationship. And if an American stayed at his hotel, then it must be a good hotel for them to spend their American dollars there.

He eventually let me talk to some of the people. Every time a guest stopped in the lobby, or any time someone even walked through, I was to ask them what time it was in English. Which I did, and in exchange for this, Mansooreh let me go outside on the steps and sniff the fresh air. He was right there next to me, though. He kept asking me where my husband was and where would I go after this? I could only tell him nemidonam (pronounced nemi-dough-man), which means, I don't know. Then telling him rafte Amrika (raft-ey), which means traveling or going somewhere in America. He shook his head and looked at me with pity and asked, "Why, Ms. Lori?"

I have no clue what the "why" implied or why he was asking me this, so I just replied, "I don't know." Maybe he thought I was bad for wanting to go back to the USA, or maybe for not knowing where my husband was.

While I was camped out in the lobby, usually all day, I took advantage of this by informing anyone who looked foreign or could speak good English to contact my parents. I met one guy from Switzerland and he was there to go backpacking. I started the conversation off by telling him to keep his passport in a safe place, and before I knew it, I had poured out my whole story and begged him to sneak me out in his backpack.

Of course, he didn't do that, but he did take down my parent's phone number and agreed to call them when he was on safe soil (out of Iran). I thanked him graciously. He also said he wasn't sure how long he would stay after listening to a story like mine.

I also met a couple from England who were somewhat uptight and cynical regarding my words, so I didn't divulge much. When the man said I was an Iranian citizen due to being married to an Iranian, and I had gotten myself into this mess, I realized it was no use to even converse with them.

I mean, let's face it, who would believe a story so far-out as mine. If I hadn't lived through it, I probably wouldn't have believed it either.

Lucky for me that Mansooreh couldn't understand much English, because if he caught onto what I was doing, he would have locked me away again.

About two weeks into my stay at the Anvari Hotel, I was restless and just wanted to be on one of those airplanes I kept hearing take off and land nearby at the airport. This was torture, and I was definitely ready to go home. I came out of my room one day and just started screaming hysterically that I was an American and I had every right to go home, why wasn't anyone helping me? Then I fell on the floor and started sobbing! I think I was close to a mental breakdown.

I was avoided by just about everyone for the next few days.

But after I tried talking to several people who were willing to listen to my tragic story and trying to get a message out to my parents, Mansooreh finally caught on to what I was doing and put me back in my room and locked it. I talked to anyone who spoke English and tried to convey to them that I was still a prisoner in the hotel, and could they email my sister, or could they call my parents when they got out of Iran? I had a few people promise to do so, but many left soon after, either frightened off by what I'd said, or maybe thinking that this hotel was housing a lunatic.

Out of all the people who I tried to relate my story to, I learned later that a few of them did get through to my mom. However, because of all these people being from different countries, like England, Australia, and Switzerland, the time differences made my mother think she was getting a rash of prank phone calls. My sister did receive an email, but she apparently didn't take it seriously.

As a last resort I asked Mansooreh that if someone could identify me and tell the Immigration Officials who I was, then would they let me go home? He said it couldn't hurt. So he set up a time when he and a woman, Ms. Anvari, the hotel owner's wife, were to take me to the Language Institute where I had taught English.

The next morning we were scheduled to go and I was so excited I could hardly contain myself. When we finally arrived at the school, I immediately saw Ms. Haghighat (pronounced Haagh-E-got). She had been the school's secretary when I worked there. I screamed her name and ran up and hugged her.

She was a bit taken aback, but she reciprocated the hugs and returned them with a smile.

The immigration people immediately began asking her if she knew me. Then I said that Bijan Pourlifahr would know me and could definitely attest to who I was. He had been the principal when I worked there and still was. I knew if Bijan showed up, I could tell him the truth of what happened and depend on him to help me. He had lived in Michigan while attending Delta College with Mohammad. I was sure he wouldn't let me down.

When Bijan came walking through the door I just about fainted. I knew he might be the one person responsible for sending me home at last, and out of this hell-hole. I screamed his name, but I couldn't hug him or shake his hand due to Islamic law. He just sat there looking at me with an expression of shock and awe on his face. His first words were, "Lori, what happened to you?"

I told him the Immigration people couldn't speak English that well and I needed to relate to him what had really happened to Mohammad and me. He sat there staring at me and couldn't believe how skinny I was. He said, "What the hell happened. There's nothing left of you!"

I told him a somewhat abbreviated story, that Mohammad and I had been in some sort of paramilitary POW camps and the only way I made it out alive was by escaping. I'd lost so much weight because of them starving me.

He shook his head, but couldn't comment because he didn't want to cause any suspicion.

Bijan asked them if I could stay with him and his wife, but they flatly refused. He then wanted to know if he could visit me at the hotel along with his wife. Again they refused. He became angry and asked them why I was being held a prisoner when I had been a productive member of their culture and taught half of its residences how to speak English. He was clearly upset, but knew when he had gone too far. Bijan knew all too well the Islamic law and its "behind closed doors" behavior.

He looked at me, just shaking his head with tears in his eyes, and said, "Lori, I will call whoever you want me to."

I gave him my mother's phone number, and asked him to call her when the time difference was to her benefit. He agreed and said he would do what he could. He had at least verified my existence, but it didn't seem to matter to the immigration people. It almost made them even more suspicious of me, for whatever reason. I didn't want to leave his familiar face behind and I tried to fill him in as fast as I could about being abducted and that I hadn't seen Mohammad since.

He said in a low tone in English, "Lori, I'm sorry. I've heard stories, but I never expected it to happen to someone I actually knew. I'm so sorry," he kept repeating. He asked me if I needed money, but Mansooreh immediately commented that everything I needed was provided for me at the hotel.

Then Mansooreh became somewhat standoffish and told Bijan it was time for us to leave.

I was so thoroughly confused, and was trying to think of what action or behavior I could have done in my past in Iran that would cause this type of punishment. I mean, my husband had evolved into someone I hardly recognized anymore and had been taken away from me. Then I was left alone in that hell camp to have horrific things happen. I was so confused and dazed that I didn't care anymore. I just sat there crying and sobbing in Bijan's office and asked him

180

what could I do to make this all better.

Upon thinking back, I had heard sketchy stories too. Mohammad had mentioned briefly once to me that his first love had been a girl named Rose in Iran. He didn't go into details, but said that they had executed her. I had tried to get details out of him, but all he had said was that for some reason both Rose and her mother had been executed shortly after he went to the USA in 1979. I assumed it had been during the revolution when the Shah was overthrown and Khomeini had been put in power. But now my gut feeling was starting to tell me that maybe there was more to my husband's past than I ever knew.

They had to physically stand me up and drag me out of Bijan's office, and I was hysterical to the point of calling them lying bastards. I reminded Mansooreh that he had said if someone could identify me that this would help. Instead it seemed to have hurt my cause. Again, I felt as if I could trust no one.

Eventually about twenty days passed of me being stowed away at the Anvari Hotel. Then came a knock on the door. I could see military boots underneath, which triggered excitement at the thought of freedom, yet also the fear of me being executed, which by now either one would have been welcomed.

Surprisingly enough, the soldier held in his hand the one thing I will never forget seeing, nor appreciate more than I had ever appreciated anything in my lifetime – that beautiful little blue book, MY PASSPORT. I was never so excited in my life.

Along with this they stated they had a signed permission slip from my husband to exit the country. This made me wonder.

Now how did they get their hands on my passport AND my husband for him to sign the permission slip? I knew then the government had something to do with my seizure at the bus station that day. I couldn't even rest assured I would get to go home. I still couldn't tell the authorities what actually happened to me, since I was sure now the government was somehow involved.

Or at least some part of it.

The soldier then asked me if I wanted to go to the Swiss Embassy in Tehran or to the USA embassy in Dubai. Well, I'd had enough of Iran at this point, so chose Dubai. The next day I was on my way!

I never questioned how in the hell they got their hands on my passport, when it had been taken from me, along with all my belongings, at the bus terminal that horrible day.

I often wonder what part Mohammad played in all this and what happened to him. I haven't seen him since the day I was taken prisoner, though later I found out he was still alive.

I felt certain by now the government must have been involved, and because of my bad luck, I was also sure the plane would probably crash on the way to Dubai.

CHAPTER 20

Out of Iran

I never found out what happened to Faresh. She went a totally different way than I did, once we were at the edge of the city. I don't think she wanted to deal with the Iranian government for help, as well. I can only hope that she is well. I never found out the fate of her brother and parents who stayed behind, either. I'm guessing that she contacted relatives who may have arranged their release through bribes or other means. As I've said before, most lower officials, and many upper officials as well, are open to bribes.

The Iranian Government paid for my airfare from Shiraz to Dubai, plus gave me an additional 1000 Tomans to use for what ever I might need. This 1000 Tomans was the equivalency of $1.25 in American money and wasn't all that useful in Persian currency either. It might have bought me a sandwich.

When I arrived at the airport in Shiraz, I noticed they had found two of my suitcases. Not much in one of them, except some picture albums I had originally brought with me to Iran with photos of my family and others, and a video of my birthday party from 1997 back in America while with Mohammad. There was also a jewelry box with a ring in it. The other had a little clothing including a dress that Mohammad said was his favorite and had bought for me. Also a bit of make up. Hardly anything that was originally packed in it. A far cry from the four suitcases we had packed full with sentimental belongings as well as gifts for our families when we first attempted to leave. However, I was just shocked to see these suitcases at all. Especially since they'd been left at the bus station. They did manage to pack my Qur'an and prayer rug, though. How nice. What good Muslims they were. I think the selected items were meant to tell me that if I wanted to keep people safe in my life, I should opt to be quiet. They were like silent threats.

The airport in Shiraz did not have a restaurant or shops or

anything like they do in the USA. Normally when your plane lands, they take you by bus from the landing field and take you to customs. That is all they have. Visitors are expected to eat downtown or go to the hotels. I didn't eat anything on the plane. The flight from Iran to Dubai was maybe an hour and a half at the most. It wasn't that far.

When I finally arrived in Dubai, I tried to see someone about getting to the American Embassy. One nice couple who was on the plane to Dubai from Iran felt pity for me when I told them my story and they gave me 11,000 Tomans to use for taxi fare and whatever else I might need. This was equivalent to about $13.75 in American money. Since I couldn't afford a hotel, I wound up spending two nights at the airport in Dubai. Even sleeping in their chairs and on the floor was not much different than sleeping in that camp. Though my back still hurt quite a bit.

At this airport, you can use a rented shopping cart to haul your belongings with, since many people have to wait a day or two for a connecting flight. I used some of the money to do this.

I met some very kind people who were there from Africa. Also, I had been observing a large family from Bangladesh who had one loud and whiney baby, which the mother breast fed without any reservations. The family seemed very poor. So, utilizing the money the couple on the plane had given me, I asked the people from Bangladesh to watch my cart of belongings so I could go downstairs and buy them some food. However, their English was nil and they didn't seem to understand what I was doing at the time.

Upon returning from the McDonalds downstairs, I brought the woman some food, since she was broke and breast-feeding. But I also brought the other members food too. They were overjoyed and wolfed down the hamburgers and fries very quickly. Since I was so used to not eating for days at a time, I didn't buy myself any food.

I then took my belongings and returned to my seat/bed at the airport. I was going through my things when I noticed a ring that I'd found in my Persian jewelry box, which the Iranian Officials had decided to include with my belongings, was missing. It was a very expensive diamond. However, diamonds were of no big deal to me when I was married to a man like Mohammad. So, when I found the ring in the jewelry box I just left it there. It had no sentimental value for me. But I figured it might come in handy later if I needed to pawn or sell it. Now it was missing.

I thought that maybe one of the members of the family from Bangladesh had taken it, since they were the ones I'd left my stuff with. I went to the airport security and reported it. They sent in the Sheik's son, but I actually think he was the Sheik. His name was Mohammad, too. He was kind, spoke excellent English, and had discovered via security video tape that the woman was the one who had taken my ring. He then became embarrassed and angry. He apologized to me and sent a police officer to arrest the woman.

They were escorting her away to <u>chop off her hand</u>! She had a choice, I think, of fourteen years in prison, or to lose her right hand.

I nearly died when I heard this. I immediately pleaded with the Sheik, that I would not press charges, nor file a complaint.

He then looked at me affectionately and let the woman go, but he continued to counsel me on what kind of person I was, that I shouldn't let people get away with a crime like this, especially in their country where they have a saying: That you can leave your briefcase on the counter and forget about it, then return two weeks later and find it still there. They have a similar saying in Iran, but not many people in authority live by it since most of my belongings were gone from my suitcases.

The Sheik then became angry at hearing my story and stormed off to the American Embassy to tell our government officials there to get off their asses and take care of me. That very day I was housed in the Astoria Hotel in Dubai, then given 50,000 Dirhams per day as an allowance. I believe this was equivalent to about $20 in US currency.

The Sheik also checked me into the American Hospital in Dubai, under another name, and had my wounds checked. I was not allowed to take my medical records with me from that hospital, nor am I able to get them now. This is why it is so hard to verify my medical treatment there. I was admitted to the hospital overnight. I was put under an anesthetic and told that internal stitches had been placed inside my uterus, but they would dissolve. They had placed IV's in me and I was able to drink water. I was also given medication for infection and treated for dehydration and malnutrition.

Even with the one bowl of rice a day for nearly three weeks at the Anvari Hotel in Shiraz, Iran, it was not enough to increase my body weight by much. This is not something you recover from overnight. I also believe part of the reason I was so malnourished was due to all the stress of trying to get out of Iran, yet still being held prisoner in the Anvari Hotel. Also, one bowl of rice a day doesn't do a lot to fatten you up in the first place.

The Sheik came to my bedside when I awoke from the anesthetic. I noticed he had tears in his eyes. He continued to tell me what a shame all of this was, and that my husband's name was on his list if he ever passed through his airport.

The Sheik was a very kind man – a very fat man – but kind and good hearted. He was probably the kindest man I'd ever met, with a heart of gold and filled with good intentions that finally led to my arrival back to the USA. Detroit to be exact.

He was respected, but did not dress traditionally in the robes, but rather wore military style attire. He asked me to stay in Dubai and get a job at the American Hospital, since I'd had my nurse's training. I tried not to hurt his feelings, by lying and saying that I needed to go home first and see my family, then I would return.

Now let me digress here a little bit. When the Sheik and his son had me picked up and taken to the American Hospital and my injuries checked, I only received the kindest most respectful treatment from both of them. In Middle Eastern countries it is very difficult for women to get treated in the manner they should since the doctors have to consult with their husbands, or the male of the family when they are taking down medical histories and signs and symptoms. It is very uncommon for the woman to talk directly to the doctor, since this would mean eye contact with a male who was not her husband. Even though this was an American hospital, they abided by the Muslim laws in Dubai. So all my history was related to the doctor <u>via a female nurse</u> that was the so called "communicator" at my bedside.

Not much treatment was done except to my female anatomy due to the rifle puncture wound. I was first given a physical of the area, then the doctor had the nurse ask me certain questions, like when I menstruated did I use tampons? Well, I never used those, but I was reading between the lines to understand where he was going with his questions. He was wondering what all the internal injuries were from. I told the nurse to tell the doctor in depth about my experience. But she said she couldn't really relate all of that for reasons I wouldn't understand. Then he told me I would need internal stitches.

They gave me a shot of something that put me out for about five hours. When I woke up, I was told that they had put in self-dissolving stitches to help the healing process, but that was about all I could get from them information wise. And to be honest, at this point, I really didn't care. I was just grateful that someone was taking the initiative to help me. I believe they also checked my feet, but these wounds had been healing on their own during my three week forced stay at the Anvari Hotel in Shiraz.

After I'd been awake for a while and they observed that I could eat a little bit and drink without vomiting, I was returned to the Astoria Hotel.

I don't know if it was the pain medication, or just the sheer excitement of finally being in surroundings that mimicked home, but I felt better than I had in a long time. The hotel was beautiful and probably one of the best by far that I'd ever stayed in. I had everything. A huge screen TV filled up one whole side of a wall. There was a bar downstairs that was also a taco bar. For reasons I didn't understand at the time, I wanted a drink. I hadn't had one in five years, not a real one at least.

Drinking is against Islamic law, as are drugs, but what goes on in public and behind closed doors are two very different things. I think that is one of the reasons so many of the men in Iran are hooked on drugs, to self-medicate, because they hate their lives and have no control over them. I'd had some home-made vodka on occasion, which is very common in Iran, but to have a drink of Jim Beam and Diet Coke, two very rare commodities in Iran, was simply too exciting to turn down while in Dubai. That, and I did have the urge to try to forget all the chaos in my life and everything that had happened in Iran. I was just trying to remember a _me_ that used to exist prior to going to Iran.

Anyway, I went down stairs to the bar and ordered a Jim Beam and Diet Coke along with some nachos. It felt like heaven, thanks to whoever was paying for my stay at the Astoria. I truly believe it was the Sheik who footed the bill, because the government would have put me a cockroach infested slum hotel near the airport like before, and probably kept me prisoner there as well. But I was allowed a credit of all the facilities within the hotel. And this was a five star hotel.

Dubai was nice. As a woman you aren't required to wear a hejab, the Muslim dress or hair covering. It is so much freer than in Iran. But then again a rat infested hole without people would have seemed nicer to me, than in Iran.

I was also allowed to use the phone from my hotel room. There were no restrictions. You can have a drink and you don't have to cover your hair. It is a very free country.

After I downed the first drink, I met some people from Britain and Australia who were there after working on breakers in the gulf. I thought they said they worked for the military, but I can't remember for sure.

One drink of the strong bourbon after a five year abstinence caught up with me. Also, I forgot that my body weight was much smaller than what it used to be. I now weighed in at about 70 pounds, if I was lucky. I loved the atmosphere there, all the different accents had me laughing. However, after the second drink, it hit me fast. I couldn't walk or see. I had to have one of the hotel assistants almost literally carry me to my room. I don't know why I didn't throw up from the liquor and the nachos. Some things made me sick while others didn't.

I phoned the Sheik's son when I returned to my room and he called me a crazy girl, since the medication was probably still in my system from the hospital, which most likely didn't mix too well with the liquor. He laughed and told me he would come by tomorrow.

* * *

The next day a consulate came and took me to the American Embassy where I signed paperwork and was told I would have to pay the US back for my plane ticket home, in the amount of $900 before my passport could be taken off restriction. Once I got to the American Embassy in Dubai, I tried to explain to them what had happened, that there were other people with US ties still being held prisoners in that camp.

But they just laughed it off and didn't take me seriously. They even acted annoyed. They didn't say much as I tried to talk, but they kept dismissing my words like they were hogwash. They eventually took me into the Embassy assistance room where I had to talk to a person through a glass partitioned window. This felt like just another type of prison environment, and their actions only made it worse. By then, it seemed like every word out of my mouth became a problem for me. I was becoming frustrated and angry that they wouldn't believe me.

Then they wanted me to sign a paper stating that I would not talk to the press, or any government officials upon my return to America – which I thought was strange. Why didn't they want anyone to know what had happened to me? And especially when they didn't even seem to believe me in the first place? They thought my story was hogwash, yet they didn't want me to tell anyone else. None of this made sense to me. Which leads me to believe that our government doesn't want the public to know the truth of what goes on in Iran. There is some type of coverup.

They made me sign it or I wouldn't be able to go home! It was an agreement that said in effect that once I got home, I wouldn't relate my experiences to anyone of what I had gone through abroad, including my time in Iran. I also had to sign an agreement that I wouldn't talk to the press or any political people upon my return home.

I asked them why I had to sign this, and what were they going to do about the other people back in that camp?

They told me in a very sarcastic tone that if there were, in fact, anyone back in this camp which I spoke of, then they would eventually be found, but Iran wasn't their main concern just then.

Now remember, this was in November of 2001, when I was at the Embassy. It was just a couple of months after the 9/11 incident, and looking back now, I can understand their haughtiness a little. I didn't know that much about what was going on at home, and didn't find out until later that the US was involved in a big search for Osma Bin Ladin and the other terrorists involved in planning the attacks on the World Trade Center Towers. But for them to act so callous about human beings who might not survive if no one came to their aid, was more than I could understand just then. While I was not in the USA during the 9/11 attacks, I was having a crisis of my own in Iran, and these American Embassy people in Dubai were leaving a rotten taste in my mouth as far as our own government was concerned.

I thought they were supposed to help our citizens who were in distress when abroad.

There was one man, named Ward, who signed my passport, and he treated me the most rudely.

He asked me many questions, like: What was I thinking when I tried to relay a story of that proportion to the first American I saw?

My response was that I was hoping to get someone to listen to me, so that maybe the others who were still there could get help.

Ward laughed and told me to relax, that I would be home soon. He never took me seriously, and every time I tried to explain things to him, he would interrupt me and tell me to save it for when I got home.

I then asked him who the hell was I supposed to tell, since his embassy made me sign a statement not to talk to anyone. He just waved his hand and said that was protocol and I should just relax.

However, after I got home to the USA, I was told that piece of paper held no weight, since it was signed in Dubai, and also under duress with the threat of not letting me leave the country to come home if I didn't sign it.

I asked Ward if the embassy was going to make me sleep at the airport again until they got me a flight home? He just said it wasn't their fault no one had notified them. My reply was that the Sheik's assistant had notified them when he first found out about me. Ward then informed me that due to the Sheik, I would be staying at the Astoria Hotel until my departure.

It was there I returned to after my time at the American Embassy.

* * *

I stayed three more nights in the Astoria Hotel. Then they came to whisk me off to the airport for America. The Sheik even paid for a doctor to accompany me while on the flight. I'd been feeling sick and running a fever. Possibly due to the internal stitches in my uterus and my body's immune system being quite low from my malnutrition. Even though I could eat whatever I wanted while at the hotel, I still didn't feel like eating much, and when I did eat, a small amount filled me up.

I called my sister from the airport in Dubai with a calling card which I had purchased with my allowance, and told her that I was coming home. I didn't phone my mother from Dubai, since I didn't think she really cared if I came home or not, due to her attitude from when I'd tried to talk to her before. So, instead, I opted to phone my Sister. I asked her if she could pick me up when I got into Detroit, and she yelled, "YES!" very enthusiastically. I can understand <u>now</u> that I'm home about my mother's skepticism at my phone calls, but I didn't then.

Later, when I talked to my sister and my mother heard that I was truly coming home, she broke down and wept. You have to remember that when I first went to Iran, I never informed my family that I was going. Mohammad and I sort of left in a hurry. I just called them a couple of weeks later and said, "Guess where I am?" Therefore, my family knew that I was a very impulsive person and often did irrational things, to say the least, but that was a humdinger even for them to digest.

I was picked up at the hotel and put on a Lufthansa flight that made a stop in Germany before it went on to Detroit.

CHAPTER 21

Headed Home

T he flight from Dubai to Germany was around six hours.
When I got to Germany where there was a layover in
Frankfurt, I was first amazed at the size of the airport. Then,
to see it had a casino in it, and people were drinking already, despite
it only being 8:00 a.m. there, was nearly unbelievable. I remember
talking to three men who were on their way to Turkey and were half
drunk on good stout German beer. They animatedly told me about
how they were looking forward to exploring the capital city of
Ankara while taking in the sights, though they hoped to catch a few
shows with belly dancers.

I thought to myself, how naive people can be. They leave their
own country to travel abroad in hopes of finding excitement and
adventure, never speculating on the horrors that might manifest
themselves. I envied those boys, yet feared for them at the same
time.

I do recall telling them to keep their passports tucked in a safe
place, because if they lost it, they would be in trouble, since in Iran at
least, if you don't have identification on you, then the police will
take you to jail. I found that out a few times during my stay in Iran.
Even Iranian citizens are forced to carry their shenas (pronounced
sha-nass), which means birth certificate in Persian. The three men
finally had to leave since their flight was being called for boarding. I
wished them well and told them to be careful, but they were too
drunk to make sense of the seriousness in my voice. Well, I thought,
no one would probably bother them, since they were MEN and
looked like upper class as well, which always helps.

When my flight was being called for boarding, I was in the
airport McDonalds, scarfing down a Big Mac. Actually trying to
taste it and enjoy it. It was the first time I'd eaten anything that heavy
and filling in nearly three months. Although my jaw still hurt and

everything else was awakening to pain, I wanted to take advantage of this one time when I could eat anything I wanted. I guessed I had probably lost close to 70 pounds due to the prison camp's weight loss program. I think grasshoppers and ants were probably zero points on this diet.

I rushed to my gate to re-board the plane and saw the doctor who had been caring for me during the flight. He told me that a Big Mac might not be the best food to be eating right then, especially since I was still ill. I assured him that I'd be fine. A half hour later I was taking up residency in the plane's lavatory. I was vomiting once more, only this time I actually had food in my stomach to vomit, rather than just dry heaves. I literally ate my words to the doctor, took care of events in the bathroom, then quickly returned to my bed which was made up on the plane. The doctor gave me that "I told you so" look, but refrained from saying anything. Dr. Ali was a kind, older man with a face like a big teddy bear. I trusted him, and he spoke English fairly well.

Here I was, fresh out of a situation that would breed distrust in anyone, yet I found it quite easy to trust this man. Maybe it was due to him taking care of me and trying to fix all those things the soldiers broke in that camp.

However, while on the plane ride home, all I could think about was how I was not ever going to allow myself to stupidly trust another relationship with a man again. I was sick as well and had a fever, so my drifting in and out were somewhat sporadic events with the "outs" being filled with dreams of my mother's tuna casserole, and my "ins" being filled with a variety of thoughts. I just couldn't comprehend the whole ordeal I'd been through and thought I was somewhat detached from reality. To this day I often feel as though I'm operating on automatic pilot, but the emotions are starting to return, as much as I dread that.

Since I had been throwing up, I didn't eat anything while on the plane as it would cause me to throw up again. Even drinking water made me throw up.

The flight from Fankfurt, Germany to Detroit lasted about eight and a half to nine hours. I slept much of the time.

Later, I heard the pilot announce that in a few minutes we would be arriving at the Detroit Metro Airport. We were in <u>my</u> country now, I thought.

Once arriving home, I went through the emotional upheaval of culture shock. Yes, I know it sounds crazy, but there was a lot of culture shock for someone who had just spent four years learning not to expose their hair, or body parts, and not to mention the dos and don'ts of the culture. That is, don't shake a man's hand when meeting him, walk behind your husband, unless he approves of you walking next to him. And so on and so on.

No one can imagine the gratefulness I experienced just being able to speak my mind once more, without fear of being punished for it. Or just the freedom to do my hair then not have to keep it hidden behind a roose-a-ree, which is what they call the scarf in Iran.

I also was not expecting so much ignorance about the Islamic religion. As I said, I really became involved in the religion to the point of praying five times daily, or doubling up on prayers in the morning to compensate for the noontime prayer when I used to teach my classes. Yes, you can do this, you can say your prayers twice in the morning to substitute for the noon prayer. Also, you don't have to pray when you're sick or traveling, if this is not feasible. The Islamic religion itself is not a BAD religion. It has many good points. The only bad things that make most of us link Islam to terrorism are the fanatics – those who take the Holy Qur'an out of context and interpret it for their own causes and justifications.

Sorry for the diversions here.

Upon arriving home, I must say that things were somewhat of a shock to me regarding events that had transpired while I was away. I found out later that Mohammad's brother, Abbas, who lived in the Untied States, had called my mom to tell her I was addicted to drugs, and if I should ever call home, it was probably to ask for money to buy drugs. And if for some reason I never came back home, it was probably due to an overdose.

So, when Faresh and I had finally sneaked into the hall at that camp to use the phone and call my mother, she'd believed Abbas' story, who was just covering his family's tracks in case I disappeared and was never heard from again. Or if I tried to get her to send me money to come home she would refuse. My mom didn't know about all the lies. Therefore when I called her for money for a plane ticket to get home while still a prisoner at the Anvari Hotel in Shiraz, she thought it was for drug money instead. That's why she treated me so badly, which she still feels guilty about to this day.

However, at the time I couldn't understand why she was so flippant and mean. Besides, it was probably about 4:00 a.m. her time when I had called and woke her up. I told her to contact the Swiss Embassy since there was no American Embassy in Iran. My mother, being a stay at home mom all her life, was very naive regarding foreign matters, let alone what would be involved in helping out her wayward daughter who was being held captive in a land such as Iran. Needless to say, my mother acted very cool through all my pleadings to get my sister to help. And she acted so nonchalantly at my crying and not wanting to get off the phone. But since it was my mother, I didn't want to part with hearing her familiar voice in the midst of what I was enduring then. As I got near the end of our conversation, I told my mother I would probably get into trouble for contacting her. Her reply was that I should get going then. I had no idea why she was so casual, but I also wasn't in the right frame of mind to sit and analyze it at the time. Of course, Faresh and I did get a beating that day.

After I returned home, though, I understood all this a lot better in retrospect. She didn't think I would really show up, figuring this was only a ploy to get drug money, so she didn't come to meet me at the airport. My parents live clear out in the middle of nowhere in the Upper Peninsula of Michigan, a good nine hours drive to Detroit, so I can't blame her for not wanting to drive that far and take the chance of me not showing up. Also, my dad was ill at the time.

Therefore, only my sister came to meet me.

It wasn't until after I got home that I found out all this other stuff.

When I arrived back in Detroit, via Lufthansa Air, I was met by an ambulance, but told them that I'd made it this far on my own two legs, and was going to walk out. What could they do but stand there and watch.

My sister was waiting for me at customs and didn't recognize me when I first emerged. I looked at her and said, "It's me, Lori!"

She just turned her head and stared at me with a look of utter shock, then tears started to stream down her face. I told her there was no reason to cry, now that I was home. She did mention that this was probably the first time in our lives when I was skinnier than her.

196

To add to my confusion, I also learned upon arriving home, that my son, Douglas, had been put in prison. I was totally shocked and angry about this. He had been living with his father, which I learned hadn't been the best decision on my behalf to allow this to happen. But then again, who knows what he might have suffered at the hands of the soldiers if he had been with me in Iran? He might have been the boy who got shot instead of the other one. But at the time I left, I didn't want to force him to move to Iran with me.

I will admit that this was my fault because I let him stay with his dad. While he was living with his dad, he was arrested for armed robbery, which got him five to fifteen years. I just couldn't fathom this. Dougie and I had been close all the time he was growing up. We were not only forced to be close due to the single parent nature of our relationship, but we were more like roommates as some people observed. He was my top priority while raising him, that and showing him that you could be a single parent and still graduate from college. This in itself is what probably strained some of the time I did have with him. Though we survived it, and he had never gotten into any legal trouble while with me. Now he was eighteen years old and had to face his own demons.

Not only did I learn that he was in prison, but that I was also a grandmother. This was yet another shock to my system, along with the food that I had the opportunity to eat now. I didn't know what to do or say, or where to start.

Now you might wonder how come I didn't know these things. When I first moved to Iran, I tried to call my family about once a week. But as time went by it became more like once a month, and by the end of the four years it was only every few months, whenever Mohammad allowed me to call. At no time did anyone in my family mention that I had become a grandmother, or that my son was in jail. Of course, the last few months I was having problems of my own. Then when I desperately did reach her by phone, she only thought I was calling for drug money.

* * *

Prior to leaving for Iran, I had a husband with a good income, I had a nursing license to provide my own income, plus I had all my personal belongings that I had acquired over the years. After returning home, I had nothing but literally the clothes on my back. I was starting over at age thirty-six.

My nursing license had been suspended due to the false prescriptions I had written before leaving the country. Charges that I had incurred prior to leaving, you might remember. In fact, it was because of these charges which encouraged me to leave America and go to Iran with my husband. Now I had no income, and no money. I was broke. It was a good thing I still had some family members who loved me.

I stayed with my sister, and we once again tried to mend our relationship. You might remember that she was the one who slept with my other husband and a previous boyfriend. The reason I didn't stay with my parents was, as I said, they lived out in the middle of nowhere and I wanted to find work as soon as possible. Also, I wanted to be closer to my son so I could visit him.

As a note here, I would like to add that my son and I regularly keep in touch by writing and I visit him as often as I can afford to on a budget like mine. I intend to assist him any way I can upon his release. His crime makes no difference in the level or degree of love I have for him. I will always love him. This is what unconditional love is all about.

During my first week back, my sister and I went to the movies and saw Joe Dirt. I about laughed my head off. It was good to just be free to do what I wanted. However, all good things must come to an end. I had no income and no money, so I had to look for work.

I eventually obtained a job and wanted to clear up my past criminal charges. I even asked at the airport customs office when I first returned to Detroit if there were any warrants for me, and they said no. So I figured they must have dropped it, or the statute of limitations had run out. Silly me!

I got a very minimal paying job due to my nursing license being suspended. I applied for my driver's license about a week after I returned home. About two weeks later I was picked up by the police at my sister's residence where I was staying. The funny thing is, and yes, I tend to have a sarcastic sense of humor, is that we were on our way home and were laughing about what we'd do if the cops came and I had to spend Christmas in jail after just arriving home from

Iran and all.

Well, you guessed it. I not only spent my birthday in jail, but Christmas, New Years, and Valentines Day as well, awaiting sentencing on charges in three counties for false prescriptions.

I tallied up a total of about four months in jail. But to me, this wasn't like jail, nor did it seem as bad after where I'd just come from. Getting three square meals a day, a bed to sleep on, TV and reading material, not to mention a real toilet you could sit on. This was more like a "time out" in a nicer environment. Sure, I missed my family, but I was used to being away from them since I was about fifteen, either due to my own actions, or because of someone else's, so I could last another few months. What did bother me was not being allowed to smoke in the jail. It was hard to get used to their "No Smoking" policy. But, I did pay my debt to society and paid for my earlier foolishness as well.

Upon being released from jail on March 15, 2002, I moved in with my birth sister. Since I had been adopted when I was six months old, I had eventually met my real brothers and sisters when I was sixteen years old. I never really considered them my family, since the ones who "chose" me were the ones who endured all the hardships with me, and put up with me, therefore I rarely kept in touch with my birth family. But I couldn't stay with my adopted sister, the one I had been living with, and the one who picked me up at the airport, since her husband was a parole officer and it created a conflict of interest with his work.

However, I wasn't happy living with my birth sister, whom I won't give out her name here, due to her psychosis – God, I hope it isn't hereditary. Talk about your schizo, psycho blissfully ignorant person. She didn't want the Qur'an in her house because some ladies from her church told her that if I prayed on the holy rug in her house, it would bring in evil spirits.

What could I do, but tolerate it until I got on my feet again.

Besides being so ignorantly swayed by the thoughts of others, she'd became a born again Christian. At the time I was also very sarcastic towards our government because of their lack of help in getting me home and their attitude when I had tried to tell them my story. I still held a lot of anger towards them. Also, for not believing that these prisoner camps exist where those with American ties might still be kept.

I exercised my right to free speech, maybe a little too much. I even joined the IPC, which stands for the Iran Politics Club, a group of freedom fighters, fighting for the wonderful, if not admirable, cause of trying to democratize Iran. The founder is a bit of a fruitcake, he's sarcastic, outspoken, but sincere to his cause 100%, and he's the one who first gave me the idea of putting my story into words.

The only reason I first joined the club was to try and find answers about my husband, and the Iran prisoner camps, and maybe get some insight into what had happened to me there and <u>why</u> I was put in that camp.

I eventually started my own political club on Yahoo called Loris Lords. The Lords stood for Logical Open Realistic Debates, and was not intended to mock any religion or politics. But to open dialogue between people.

I can honestly tell you that I sometimes miss Iran to this day. Yes, I know what happened to me there was hideous, but the Persians are some of the nicest and kindest people I've ever met – excluding my husband Mohammad and his family of course.

The land and its history is rich and beautiful and if things could ever work out between our two governments, that country would be a gold mine for tourism.

After the initial shock of arriving home and dealing with my family and all, I began questioning many things. Like how could a man like Mohammad have treated me so well and loving while in the USA, then change so drastically in his home country? I can understand it up to a point. I'm not saying it's excusable, but I understand the pressure he was under from his family and friends to keep his American wife under control, to prove that he could, as a Muslim and a man, control someone who was so apt to be outspoken. And boy, did he get pressure from his family.

As I said, I also had to deal with the fact that my son was in prison, and that I was a new grandmother of a bouncing baby grandson.

I tried to put the events which happened in Iran out of my mind and dismiss them like a bad dream. But it wasn't that easy. Nightmares became imminent any time my eyes stayed closed for any length of time. Therefore, my cure for this was to simply not sleep. Which worked for about the first six months after I was home. However, you can only go so long before you have sleep deprivation.

A few people have hypothesized that my escape was not due to any real luck at all. One friend of mine, Ed Monagin, an old friend of the family's, is a retired military man who used to guard snipers in Viet Nam. His take on this is that whoever had us, knew someone had been calling from the USA and inquiring into my whereabouts in Iran. Faresh also had family in the USA who may have made inquiries too. The soldiers who held us thought it might be best to let us go. But how could they do it and still maintain their reputation? Or at least not get into trouble with their superiors? By letting us think we escaped. Which in reality does not sound that bizarre. Ed is also the one who helped me understand some of the art of psychological warfare. He said the public rapes were supposed to isolate the prisoners from each other, so that we were too ashamed to try to communicate with anyone there. Which it did work to some extent, as we were too ashamed to look at the others afterward. Ed has been a great supporter of mine, and I owe him much thanks and gratitude.

It's possible that many of the prisoners who were taken out of the camp at various times had bribed the guards or higher ranking officers into releasing them. As I've mentioned before, bribes are common in these countries where soldiers are poorly paid and poverty is rampant.

* * *

When I returned home, the only thing I can tell you is I thought I could mentally get over all the pain and the experiences of that camp on my own. I felt that no one would understand what I went through. Even with talking to those psychologists who deal with rape victims . . . well, I couldn't understand how someone could help me with a problem if they've never experienced it themselves. And rape alone is a horror undefinable in a universal term, but rather, a wholly individual experience. No two rapes can be viewed the same, nor felt by the victims the same way.

I thought the rapes I went through would be totally

uncomprehensible to anyone in a support group, since not many people in that group would have endured copious amounts of the act in a POW camp in Iran. So I succumbed to the idea that no one would be able to understand it, and therefore it was up to me to get over it by myself and get on with my life. After all, that was in the past, and this was now. No matter who I talked to, or what I did, I couldn't change what had already happened to me, so I just adhered to the principle that this would be an experience to let go of and not ponder too deeply. This and the underlying fear that if I ever did start to feel sorry for myself, or dwell on the horrific acts I actually went through over there, that I would lose my sanity all together and wind up in some rubber room for the rest of my life.

When I came home, I kept up a strong front for my family's sake. I kind of adopted a sarcastic sense of humor in order to deal with things, and have since started seeing a therapist for the Post Traumatic Stress Disorder I have been diagnosed with. Therefore, I started therapy near the end of 2002. But my stubborn side still told me I don't have PTSD, that it was just a diagnosis they felt obligated to slap on me due to the events in Iran. I still suffer from periods of smelling strong unpleasant odors that are exactly like the ones I'd smelled in the camp, like fish or mortar fire.

While in the camp they used to have practice exercises in the distance, or else someone was bombing another area and not telling us, but you could hear the bombs at night and sometimes see them go shooting through the air. When I first returned home, I almost had a breakdown during a real bad thunderstorm. It brought back sounds that were all too familiar, as well as my old fear of the lightning. I have now gotten over that, I think. The smells I have not, though. Often an odor will trigger something in me and bring back memories of the camp.

Though Chris, my therapist, is a good listener, it has been hard for her to help me. She has been a bit befuddled at times since she has never had a patient like me seek counseling from her. I think sometimes she kept seeing me just to solve her curiosity about what happened, besides, she kept hoping she could help me.

I still can not sleep through the night and no matter what time I go to bed, or how tired I am, I manage to wake up every night around 3:00 a.m. I have no idea of the significance of this.

I had really bad nightmares any time I fell asleep the first two years after I returned. This is probably why I trained my mind to believe sleep was not good for me. But again, my nightmares are becoming farther and fewer between now.

CHAPTER 22

The Aftermath

First off, I want to digress a bit here and allow you some insight into an average day in the prisoner camp and what it was like, not only for me, but also for all others there.

Usually I did not sleep much, maybe I would catch a few minutes here and there, but that was it. Sleep was very sporadic. The only time I got any real rest was when I was knocked unconscious from my beatings, or sometimes passed out after a forced heroin injection in my gums. But I would listen to the soldiers speak Farsi together, also at times Arabic, and try to make heads or tails out of what I could hear, then fill in the gaps with what I couldn't.

In the mornings there would usually be a changing of the guard, so to speak, and they would laugh at or mock whatever event they had caused to happen the night before. They would laugh and point to one of us to humiliate us. It was then that I realized there was no such thing as every human being possessing a humane or kind inner core.

I felt dirty, but not in the physical sense you might think, although none of us had taken showers, or ate much in weeks. It wasn't the kind of dirtiness that you feel from not washing.

It was an inner feeling that made me constantly want to vomit, or have an exorcism performed. Either way, that unpleasantness bothered me the most. When you're placed in a life or death situation, you do what you have to do, whether it is against your morals or not; your only motivation is to survive the ordeal.

Well, I did survive. I tried to obey the soldiers as best I could, and not put up too much of a fight. At first I fought like a panther whenever they came to take me away to rape me, or to inject the heroin in my gums. But after a while you lose your will to fight, since you know it is going to happen anyway, no matter how much you object. They did everything they could to break my spirit.

I learned to just disassociate from the whole scenario and think back to a time when things were better. Or make believe that by doing what they wanted it might get me home quicker, or that this could be the last time something so degrading would happen to me. I learned, also, that trust is not a given, nor is it earned indefinitely. I learned not to be as trusting as I was when I first arrived in Iran.

I was with my husband, Mohammad, for nine years altogether and thought I could trust him, but, boy was I wrong! You would think that after that long you could trust a person – not so. And as for anyone marrying an Iranian, Middle Easterner, or for that matter, anyone from a different culture than yours, I strongly suggest learning as much about that culture as possible. Don't be prejudiced or shun a relationship due to the differences of the two cultures, but don't fall hook, line, and sinker, and delve into anything without thoroughly researching it first either.

Love is a wonderful thing, but can be very deceptive, and vague upon the surface when you think you have fallen head over heels for another. So give yourself time, and listen to the experiences of others before committing yourself to a situation that you may regret later. That was my downfall, I didn't listen to the warnings of others. Mohammad's first wife, who I'd been acquainted with, tried to warn me, but then she was even taken in by him again after she left him. He was a master at manipulation.

Don't get me wrong, I have nothing against two cultures, races, or religions mixing and getting married. But I do when it comes to one being ignorant and just listening to the words of their supposed loved one, and loyally, unquestioningly, jumping in feet first. Had I listened to Betty Mahmoody's story of Not Without My Daughter more closely, then I would have been more cautious than to go to a strange land based solely on what my hubby had told me. Which was: Iran has changed, it's more modern, they don't treat women like that anymore, blah, blah, blah! While I admit that Persians are some of the kindest people I know, I can also tell you that they are some of the most manipulative. But this is not their fault, this is their training from birth. They are never allowed to express their true emotions. Also due to being punished for it, or for reasons that might infringe on the family's reputation in society.

Now getting back to the camp . . . yes, I do have a tendency to stray on subjects and I apologize for this. A little hope built up in my mind every morning. The hope that today was the day I was going to be freed, but I would eventually start doing my ant study once again. Which meant staring at an ant hill and watching the ants march in and out of their hill while carrying something . . . I don't think it was food, because if it had been, I would have been the biggest thief amongst the ants, and they probably would have relocated. To be honest with you, I don't know what the hell they were taking in and out of their nest, maybe stray grains of sand, but it was more interesting to watch these insects than to see all the desperate and miserable faces of the other prisoners in the camp.

I would think for a while what it might be like to be home, to be sitting down with my parents in their living room and watching CNN. Don't ask me why, but this thought, along with my mother's tuna noodle casserole, is what kept entering my mind the most. This and killing the bastard soldiers one by one, after humiliating them, the same way they had stripped us of our own pride. Despite a person's persona in life, this can be subject to change due to the circumstances they are placed in.

After a few hours, the soldiers would take turns at getting their fringe benefits. This would be raping the girls. Then there would be the usual screaming, hysteria, and people shouting. I would also try to block this out, and try to rationalize. That there had to be people in other parts of the world who were going through much worse. But what could be worse than being starved, tortured, and raped on a daily basis? I did not have a clue, but I had to rationalize it all, just to stay sane.

Then came the dead silence after a few hours in which I would reflect on what had just happened, and worry that it would all be repeated in a few hours or the next day. I would have my moments of tears, and wonder why God had allowed this to happen to me. Hadn't I always prayed to him, talked to him, and believed without question?

I tried to think of what I had done so terribly wrong in my past to bring this grief upon myself. Well, okay, maybe I was a little headstrong in my youth and had caused my parents quite a bit of grief, but whatever I'd done it shouldn't have caused me this much punishment.

I would see others praying to Allah aloud, only to be punished more by the guards. Which led me to at first think how brave these people were, to continue believing in a faceless God, and in a God who was allowing this to happen to them. Towards the end I just thought it was pure stupidity to keep praying, and ended up despising them.

I have no clue as to why I despised them. I guess it was just one of those unexplainable emotions you cannot figure out, why you ever hated those who were in the same situation as you. Nevertheless, I did. I hated them for causing more contention than was necessary, and possibly hated, if not envied, their devoted faith in a God who I deemed had let me down, or maybe never existed in the first place.

At night, we would all watch the soldiers eat while our own stomachs grumbled and cramped with hunger, then they would smoke their opium so they could temporarily escape the life they hated as well.

I don't know which I craved more, the food or the heroin injections, to be totally honest with you, since the soldiers would give us the heroin injections involuntarily for a few days, then stop giving them to us, thus making us go through withdrawals. There were times I may have desired the heroin more than the food, since at least the heroin allowed my mind an escape of sorts, or so I thought. Plus it gave me a reprieve from all the pain of the tortures I'd suffered. The guards would demand that we all shut up while they enjoyed their festivities of the moment, which was to return to the cement building enclosure, the one with actual walls and a roof – and a telephone.

What I wouldn't have done to get in there for one night and not sleep outside in the dirt with whatever insects crawled over me and bit me, and to just be clean <u>inside</u> as well as out. So here you have a typical day: Starvation, rapes, humiliation, and always questioning your past, and faith, not only in God, but in your future as well.

Did I even want to continue living in this world knowing that there were actually people like these soldiers doing these heinous things to their supposed Muslim brothers and sisters? Could I live with this fact, now that I had actually experienced it?

It's totally different when you sit at home and hear about it on the news. It's too far away from here to be a reality, but when you live through it, you begin to question <u>everything</u> in life. It was the <u>Whys</u>? <u>What's</u>? And always the <u>Who's</u>? that bothered me. Like, why was this happening? The answer for me was, "Does it really matter, since you probably will never learn the truth anyway?" I don't know if I am making sense right now, but I am just trying to summarize how, and what I felt while I was there. Some of these questions bothered me then, and still do. Why is it that some countries can get their soldiers motivated for martyrdom and other countries can't even do what is necessary for survival, even if the equipment is there? I have no clue what the answer is here. But in that camp I came to the conclusion that whatever great answer it was they were looking for, they were not going to find it here on Earth. I was at an all time low when I was thinking about all this. But then again, upon returning home, I had the same thoughts resurface. So, go figure.

* * *

I did finally spend some time with my parents, but it wasn't until after I'd served my time in jail. It was great seeing them. I spent about a week with them. I had gained a little more weight by then, so they weren't too frantic when they saw how thin I was. And yes, I finally got to eat some of my mother's tuna noodle casserole once again, since I'd thought about it so often while being deprived of food during my stay in that camp. I didn't go back to live with my parents since they lived so far away and I had a job near my birth sister's house.

I have recently started suffering from seizures which I'm sure have a lot to do with being kicked in the head so many times during my stay in the camp. The moment the first one started was very horrific to me. I felt like I just might die at any moment. It was strange to feel that way after all the other horrors I'd been through. I couldn't talk and could barely move. They would last about two to three minutes, but seemed so much longer. Even after the seizure subsided, I couldn't function mentally. If someone spoke to me, I could hear them, but I couldn't answer them. I am taking medication now which seems to help. The doctors say the seizures could be caused by a number of things, but are most likely a delayed reaction to my head injuries while in the camp. It's really the only explanation I can figure out, since I still have the boot indentations in my skull.

When I first got home, I couldn't afford any dental work since I didn't have any money. I did have a bit of dentistry done at The University of Michigan Dental School where the students can work on you for much cheaper, but they didn't do any cosmetic work. Just fillings and pulled several broken teeth.

* * *

Just to update you, Mohammad contacted my mother by phone in January of 2002. He kept asking for her help to get him out of Iran. But when he gave my mother a cell phone number to contact him back, it didn't work. So, I knew that he was at least alive and still in Iran. Then I received a few weird phone calls again at my mother's house, but the person wouldn't leave their name, they just said they were calling from Canada. I think Mohammad had relatives or contacts in Canada. He also tried to leave voice mails for me at my sister's house in April or May of 2002, in which she contacted me and told me the number to access her voice mail so I could listen to them and determine if it was really him. It sounded like Mohammad and he just said he needed help with his Visa, but never left me a phone number for further contact.

Then I received several emails in May or June of 2002 and also a death threat video of a taped execution of a woman for adultery, in which I gathered he was subliminally telling me this could be me, since he accused me in those emails of being with someone else. They were videos you could watch online. When I finally decided in December of 2002 that it was time to move on with my life, I begged him by email for a divorce, but he kept trying to get me to come back to him. He would at first use words like, "Lori, Darling. Are you ready to come home?" And try to sweet-talk me.

But when that failed, he would use threats, like, "No one leaves Mohammad! You will remain my wife or I will kill you!"

I answered over the email, "I got your death threat video. How nice to send that to the supposed love of your life."

His answer: "I will intercept you one way or another, willing or not. You will return to your rightful owner, and yes, you will have to be beaten, but I won't execute you if you return ASAP. If you don't come, I will send someone to kill you and your family."

I finally went to the courthouse to ask how I could get a divorce from my husband with him not being in the country and explained the situation to them. They told me I could do all the paperwork for free if I copied the originals at the library which were on file. I had to file an alternate service request, which meant that I had to announce my filing of the divorce in some public paper, in the legal news section for a period of three weeks. Then once the sixty days had passed from the time I had filed the papers, I could ask for the final judgement of divorce. Thankfully I was able to obtain a divorce from him without him being here.

* * *

When I had times to myself and was alone, I would often sit and ponder my future. I really had absolutely no inclination of ever becoming involved with a man again. I had, in my mind, succumbed to a life of being single and was only here to emotionally support my son with his crisis and help him with his life. Those were my initial plans anyway.

In April of 2002, about five months after returning home, I met a man named Carl. Upon our first meeting, I was drawn to him like a magnet. As a matter of fact, without any reason whatsoever, I wanted to go home with him and just live out the rest of my life with him after our first encounter. He had no idea I felt this way. I used to leave him little messages on his computer with hints that I was drawn to him. These were on Yahoo Messenger or other emails. But I was very insecure and felt that no man would ever want me again after all the rapes and degradation I'd been through. I had decided my fate would be a life of aloneness. However, I felt so comfortable talking to Carl, and I thought he understood everything I was feeling yet so afraid to disclose. He finally caught on after a few weeks of subtle hints in his emails and asked me out. Not a big date, just a simple trip to the park where we walked and talked, then back to his

house for coffee. I won't go into details, but let's just say that on April 25, of 2002, I moved in with him, and on April 25, 2003, on the anniversary of the day I'd moved in with him, I married him.

While I don't want to go into specifics, I do want to elaborate that while Carl was my night In shining armor at the time I needed it; I didn't realize at the time that I was just looking for a man to accept me without any judgements. It wasn't soon after our marriage had begun that we both realized that we were not in love. Don't get me wrong we fought like a married couple, but in no way were caught up in the type of love that a man and woman should have. We both succumbed to this and lived for the next several years as husband and wife but in name only. We became companions and he was my sounding board for this book. He also helped me and tried to understand the problems that I suffered from relating to my time in Iran. He is a good man and we are amicable to this day. Matter of fact he allowed the marriage to continue so that I could benefit from his insurance until my disability came through and I would have Medicare. For that I am truly grateful and admire his loyalty towards helping me while I was in a "BAD" situation.

He has helped me overcome many of my fears and the hangups I had returned with. He has been nothing but supportive, has never pressured me, never made me feel like less of a person due to the actions I endured while in Iran. Though he didn't always understand my behavior, he was always willing to try. He never raised his hand or his voice to me.

As I said, I can't explain what came over me when I met him, but whatever it was, it must have been a mutual friendship and deep caring between two individuals who were drawn to each other for reasons that aren't always understood until later in a relationship.

For whatever reasons, and however it happened, I can honestly say that Carl was a Godsend at a time when I was lost and needed understanding. Thank you Carl!

I still have nightmares occasionally, and as I said, I'm currently being treated for Post Traumatic Stress Disorder as well as occasional seizures. Which leads me to how I met the TRUE LOVE OF MY LIFE…John Hinderer!

John had a John Deere dealership in the town that I was living, at the same time I had a girlfriend named Jenny who was good friends with John. To make a long story short Jenny introduced me to John but not for the purpose of dating each other, it was under other circumstances all together. But when John looked at me I felt a feeling that I hadn't ever had!....I was never sure how falling in love felt since I had been looking for men all my life and fell in love with the idea that they could protect me and was under the influence that they possibly loved me for reasons other than sex. Since being molested by my brother at age 10, and feeling isolated from my father while growing up, the only love I was looking for was the kind that told me "Lori they love you for you and want to protect you from your brother and be that father that you never had while growing up" So I never truly understood what REAL LOVE FELT LIKE.

But I did NOW! But I took it slow I didn't want to misunderstand any feelings that I was having like I did with Carl's and I relationship. That is why poor John had to be so persistent at trying to get me to go out with him. I avoided him like the plague since I was convinced that I must be feeling that same old misinterpreted kind of love, yet the feeling was different. I don't know if I can describe it accurately but the feeling s I had when I was with him were: safety, security, non-judgmental, consistency and his eyes told me that he wasn't just looking at my breast! Not to mention the heart palpitations that I suffered everytime I saw him or knew that I would be seeing him. I would get so anxious when I seen his truck around town that I'm lucky I didn't get into an accident . No this feeling for me was a first but not welcomed with opened arms. I had been in so many relationships in my life that how could I trust my feelings now??

After John had come over to my house on a daily basis and I kept ignoring his knocks at the door, he finally got fed up one day and yelled outside the door, "I'M COMING IN"! I was petrified because I still had my pajamas on and no make-up, and just felt like the ugliest person in the world. And the first thing he did was come over and give me a hug and told me that I looked just as beautiful as I was on the day I met him. So FINALLY I GAVE IN...and the rest is history. .

On a humorous note here, in the past I was accustomed to being with men who were more prone to wild activities in life. Now I can proudly say that I'm with a man who has had the same job going on twenty years, and is consistent in his behavior, does not drink or do drugs. And has no felonies or priors on his record! My family is awestruck at my good fortune and sometimes might wonder when I will blow this relationship by internally combusting due to all the consistency and calmness in my life.

For whatever reasons, and however it happened, I can honestly say that John has been my true reward for all the pain and hardships I have endured in my life. And he was well worth the wait!

John has sold his partnership in the John Deere Dealership that he had, and has stayed home with me for the past 3 yrs. To take care of me. I can't drive due to seizures yet need to go to Henry Ford Hospital on a regular basis to see my neurologist and therapist. John drives me weekly and sometimes twice weekly which is about 150 miles roundtrip. He NEVER COMPLAINS! He is there for me in the middle of the night when I wake up from a nightmare. He suffered through my manic episodes since being diagnosed with Bi-polar in 2005. He has suffered with me through my bouts of depression and suicide attempts. All without complaining. He took out loans to get my teeth fixed: that were practically all knocked out when I returned from Iran.

He has literally dedicated his life to helping me get better and become the human being that he says he knows exist behind all the trauma that I've suffered in life. He has never once hit me or even attempted to , he barely raises his voice and is ALWAYS THERE WHENEVER I NEED HIM. He honestly is MY NIGHT IN SHINING ARMOR, not just for the moment but for what I hope will be all eternity!

* * *

The strangest thing happened recently. One of the girls who I taught English to while living in Iran contacted me by email. Her name is Afsaneh Milad, and she told me she is now living in the United States, in Atlanta, along with her parents who own a couple of businesses, and she is attending college. What is strange is that she contacted me through an old email address which I had used while living in Iran, but hadn't used in years. And after our email conversation, I haven't been able to access that same email address again. But I did give her my new email address so we could stay in contact.

214

During our messages, I told her about what happened to me, and that I had not seen Mohammad again since being taken prisoner in the camp, although, he did contact me by email. She also sent me a recent photo of her. It was good to hear from someone who knew me while living in Iran. It is strange how small the world can be. But she didn't seem all that surprised at my story.

She told me that there was no secret police in Iran, but if there were, she didn't believe these groups were legal. However, she did believe there were individual terrorist groups who might have been taking anyone with American ties. Who have their own agendas and "Nonsense goals," as she called them. Those who were motivated by hatred and prejudice.

Afsaneh said that she and her family planned to stay here in the USA and apply for citizenship. They like living here and feel safer.

* * *

I just wanted to bring up something here that was pointed out to me during an online chat with some other women who'd had bad experiences with Middle Eastern men. hadn't thought of this until one of them mentioned it. That Mohammad had to have arranged for our passports <u>at least thirty days in advance </u>in order to leave the country, since it takes that long to get clearance for passports and for them to be available. <u>Therefore, he had to have known at least thirty days in advance that something was going to happen on 9/11</u>. After the United States was attacked, he made it look like our leaving was a spur of the moment decision. As these women pointed out to me, there is no way you can get passport clearance the same day as you want to leave.

Also, if you'll remember, he had a passport with another man's name on it. I never could figure out why he had this fake passport. You might remember, he told me to get rid of it when he saw the convoy trucks pull up at the bus terminal.

During our email communications, Mohammad never did explain to me what happened to him or <u>where he was</u> during the time I was held in the camp, being starved and raped. He would only say things like, "You deserved what happened to you for being an un-obedient wife." Then he called me a whore and other derogatory names. All the while trying to talk me in to going back to him.

But after pondering over the incident of our trying to leave Iran the day after 9/11, it leads me to believe that Mohammad was <u>hiding much more</u> from me than I ever thought. <u>How did he know at least thirty days ahead that something was going to happen?</u> To this day I can only speculate. Maybe someday I'll be able to find out more answers.

CHAPTER 23

Remembering

Sometimes when September rolls around, I think back to being in the camp. There are still things I think of and say, "How could this happen, and will anyone understand why?"

People think that if I just go to a therapist it will make it all better. I will become adjusted again. Unless a therapist has gone through all this, how can they possibly understand? It's not like going to a therapist who deals with rape victims on a daily basis. This was not just rape. It was pure hatred, and it wasn't by any one person. There were many who looked at us and thought of their own insecurities and their hatred for America, which was taken out on us. With many of the injuries I received, I'm still amazed to this day how or why I survived them. I'm not stronger than anyone else. I just had the will to survive, even though that was slowly draining out of me toward the end.

I recall telling Faresh that we could go a lot longer without the scraps of food than we could without water. Therefore, we focused on the water whenever they hosed us off. We would drink from the puddles until we could taste mud in our mouths. Then we would suck the moisture out of our clothes.

I remember one time, laying beside Faresh after a hosing down and looking at the bottom of her pant legs and just wanting to suck on the ends that were still wet. But I didn't, because in my mind I felt like I would be stealing something from Faresh.

Even though I try to present a strong facade to people, I have survived four years with all the after effects of what happened, and I tell myself that I'm doing well. Then all of a sudden I will want to crawl under something and isolate myself from everyone because I feel so ugly and used and disgusting. I doubt I will ever rid myself of these feelings.

I often think of Faresh and wonder if she is still alive, if her brother and parents were rescued. I think of the other people in the camp and wonder about their outcome. I sometimes just want to die inside because I will never forget what some of those people went through and will never escape the hell in my mind.

Did that father do something so terrible to the Islamic religion or the Iranian government that they felt that shooting his son in front of him was more punishment than killing the father?

I live in a surreal world most of the time. I often feel like I'm not even there and that I'm watching things from some far corner in the ceiling. I'm not sure if this is caused by the dirtiness I feel inside, and I don't want to be around other people because I'm afraid they will see all the dirtiness too.

There was a moment after the rifle barrel injury occurred and the guards were carrying me back to my spot in the camp. One of the soldiers brushed the back of my leg in an almost kind gesture. I wept, not due to my injuries, but because someone had shown me a bit of kindness. I wanted so much for someone to put their arm around me and tell me everything would be okay, and it would be over soon. In a situation like that, a little compassion goes a long way.

That soldier became special to me. Not because I enjoyed the pain and suffering, but because amidst all the screaming and the blood, and not knowing if I would make it through another day, I had a kind hand touch me, which meant <u>everything</u> to me at that moment.

The abuses became like a daily routine of sorts. It just happened and you knew it was going to happen, and we couldn't talk to each other after the event, so my mind became conditioned to not even looking at Faresh when one of us were brought back to our spot. At first I tried to use facial grimaces to communicate how sorry I was when something happened to her. But at some point I decided it was a waste of energy, since it all happened to me too.

I read about Sean Penn's <u>one day</u> in Iran and just laughed. Did he think that going to Iran as a movie star that the people would even dare come out of the closet and beg to be escorted to the USA? Most Iranians are so jealous of our freedoms that they will do almost anything to get here. Even with all the hatred they show toward us. However, if they talk about wanting to come to the USA openly they can be sent to prison or worse.

There are many women in Iran who are tortured for the sins of their husbands. I'm talking about pregnant women who are taken to camps or some other place and have their baby cut out while the woman lies there to die a slow death while holding some form of a fetus. I learned some of these stories while teaching the English classes, since the women felt they could trust me. Women are constantly walking on egg shells in Iran. They do love their husbands, but at the same time they do not know if they can trust him. So many of the men are just unstable emotionally. They can love you to death – literally. I often saw women who had reached their breaking point and finally yelled at their husbands. I witnessed the man come right out into the street and grab the woman by the hair and actually pull her to the other side of the street. No one dared interfere or they could possibly pay with their life. The men have all the legal rights there.

* * *

Not too long ago I had a sort of breakdown. At first it seemed like one of the seizures I'd been having, but I think it was more of a mental or nervous breakdown. As I've mentioned, I really hated seeing a psychologist to deal with the aftereffects. I had gone to my regular doctor about a urinary tract problem. When I was walking out of my doctor's office, I told my friend John, who took me there, that I was feeling weak. Then all of a sudden I fell to the floor and couldn't talk. One of the nurses came out to where I was and called 9-1-1. Apparently she had a son who had seizures and said his never went on this long, nor the way mine was happening. The ambulance came and took me to the University of Michigan Hospital.

Apparently I became unruly and was trying to hurt myself, though I don't remember any of this. My friend told me that when the EMTs went to put me in the ambulance, I grabbed his leg and held on for dear life and it took two or three people to pull me away from him. He said I had the saddest, most confused look on my face and it appeared like I was fighting for my life.

When my husband, Carl, got there, he said that at least for two hours, I was speaking in Farsi and mentioned names like Mohammad, and Faresh. He said that when anyone tried to touch me I would jerk away and yell, "I'll be good, I promise. Don't hit."

My husband told me that when I was trying to talk to Faresh, I would whisper and tell her to be quiet. Then I would try to fight when someone touched me. I spend about four to five hours in this condition, basically reliving my time in the camp and in Iran.

They eventually had to paralyze me to keep me from fighting them and stuck a breathing tube down my throat and do lumbar punctures. I was there for seven days. Apparently I woke up at one point during the treatment, but I was paralyzed and couldn't let them know I was conscious. I felt everything they did to me, I heard the conversation of the doctors and interns. I couldn't even open my eyes to signal them. It was like being tortured all over again.

I let them know later when I was able to communicate that I had been conscious for part of the treatment and repeated their conversations to each other while working on me. I was not supposed to feel anything, but I did, though I could not tell them at the time due to the paralysis. I hope they will be more careful the next time they do these types of procedures to make sure the patient is actually unconscious and not just unable to move or talk due to the paralyzing drugs they give them.

* * *

What do I remember most about all that happened? The soldiers, the chaos, the confusion, the stripping of all human dignity and the true face of humility. But most of all the one true moment in my life when I was completely left alone by everyone, including my own government which had promised me "liberty and justice for all," when I was a child and innocent. While in the camp, all innocence was lost and I was completely alone to fend for myself, to depend on my mind, my strength, and most of all, my will to survive, which meant patience.

I also remember facing many facets of death's door, no grim reaper, just the games, mind-games, the Rules, or in their case, the lack of rules. The betrayal by people whom I once considered as my "brothers" and "sisters." Even my husband Mohammad who had promised to love me. The total barbarism and primitiveness seen in the guard's laughing eyes as they continued to repeatedly carry out their justifications of revenge with the "Big Satan" (what terrorists like to call the USA). Only their justifications were being executed not on the whole, but only on the part, of what I used to think of myself and the other girls as. I felt I'd been betrayed by my country and theirs. No solace for this act would ever become part of me if I survived. As the barbaric acts continued daily and repeatedly, my mind drifted back to a time in my past. I was eleven years old and it was Christmas.

While the soldiers continued their rapes, my mind drifted. It was my only escape from all the torture.

Where was God now? I asked. Long ago, at eleven, I thought he was there with me, then. I also remember the ability the mind has to succumb to automatic pilot when the body shuts down and vice versa. Within this irony I tried to plan for the future, when in all actuality my body was near death; and how to trudge on when my mind had escaped the horrors of the body's entrapment.

Also, seeing that family ties do matter when a man named Abbey, "the lovely one," sacrificed himself to stay behind with his parents who were too sick to make the journey to freedom upon escaping, and allow his sister and I to be freed.

The longest days for me was September 9th and 10th, of 2001, as I awaited the horrors of Afghanistan to "attack" the USA, knowing something terrible might happen, yet not being allowed to call home to warn family and loved ones. Survivor's guilt is hideous and sometimes harder to bear than the actual afflictions. If **I** knew two days ahead of time, why didn't our government figure it out? I couldn't have been the only one to hear about these rumors in Iran.

I miss how total self-reliance was taught to me by people who knew not my native tongue nor knew me as their sister, but as a friend, who were kind, caring, and yes, even loving, knowing not if they would survive one more day, yet still were strong in their faith in a faceless God, one whom I deemed had let me down. What courage they had!

* * *

This is my life now, and I make the decisions which I am forced to live with. I wrote a quote for my Yahoo profile and this pretty much sums it up: "While Terrorism is a war that starts developing within the mind, religion is a war that antagonizes our conscience, but love is a war within the heart!"

When we feel loved by someone important then infatuation sets in blinding us to the reality of life, a surreal seen and want to be seen effect/affect is evident. This is the life I led with Mohammad. But when your true inner spirit bonds with another human being, you not only lock the feelings of your hearts but you know deep within that what you feel is REAL! This is the life I lead now with John. I cannot express the gratitude that I feel in words for this man who has not only shown me love in return but has given me his time and finances to help me with my injuries that I sustained in Iran.

I know have my teeth back that I lost in Iran, partially from being kicked in the face, and one incident I clearly remember is:

They had put clamps on our jaws when they raped us and every time we made a sound they would tighten the clamp, I lost almost all my back teeth during that episode. I have scars on my cheeks in the shape of the clamp as well.

But these superficial scars are not deterrents to John's affections for the physical attributes that I have or have lost. He does not look at my scars, and if he does he sees past them to the person that he loves within.

We both have learned a lot, me about love and unfortunately for him, he has learned more than his past yearnings were for disorders such as PTSD, bi-polar, seizures....the list continues, but so does his love for me.

That John Deere Dealership he was part owner in, he sold it, now he is home full time to shuttle me back and forth to Henry Ford Hospital for medical and psychological appointments. He has devoted his love and time to helping me get better and to understand that he will love me no matter what and that I should trust that love to last forever. My insecurities that were evident upon entering into this relationship have waned and now I know that this man should have been the first man of my life and the only man.......but.....they say circumstances happen for reasons. I truly hope this experience as well as this book will help another girl out if she decides to travel to a foreign country without gaining knowledge beforehand. I leave you with a suggestion....Get the Jeff Bates CD, pay special close attention to the song ...THE ONE...

222

So, you see, you can suffer greatly, but still find a little happiness in the end!

For all those who suffered on 9/11/01, I say <u>GOD BLESS YOU AND MAY ALL OF US LIVE IN PEACE , IF NOT NOW, THEN SOMETIME SOON – WHEREVER THAT MAY BE!</u>

Epilogue

After I returned home, I had a lot of surgery done on my teeth that were kicked out, and on my jaw, and have remained for the most part quiet, until now.

As for me, I never appreciated setting foot on American soil as much as I did on November 14th 2001. As I've mentioned before, there was an ambulance waiting for me at the Detroit Metro Airport, but which I kindly declined. When they escorted me out of the customs area, my sister did not recognize me, due to all the wounds, broken teeth, and severe malnutrition, but when I declared, "it's me, Lori!" she broke down and cried, and we hugged like never before.

I will never forget the devotion, love and worry that my family endured, especially after my mom received my phone calls and could not acquire help from any government authorities. They told her it had been my choice to go to Iran in the first place, so it was up to me to get out. I realize our government can't just enter a foreign country to search for missing Americans without some kind of authorization from the host government. But, I still felt there was much more that could have been done to help those being held captive there. And the way they dismissed my story at the American Embassy as hogwash made me angry. To me, this tells me there are things going on that our government doesn't want the public to know about.

The true heros here are my family members. They were the ones who withstood the unknowing and the horror of their imaginations. I, on the other hand, am just a survivor, here to share my story in the hopes that something like this will never be repeated in the future. By any government.

I would like to add here a poem written by my son, Doug, of his feelings of what I endured.

REPLACEMENT!

For everything you've put people through,
For everything you've been through
You've made your bed, or so they say
But what I say is, "Hey!"
Nobody deserves this, regardless of what they say!
Sometimes I used to lie awake
Wondering what you were doing half way across the world
And now that I've learned all this My heart and soul begin to shake
So as I sit here and contemplate
What I could have done
I realize it makes no difference in our fates
The damage has been done.
As sure as I'm sitting here in prison
As this is part of my life
You have your own prison
Of sadness, grief, and strife.
We both have categories
Named so very true
But nothing better describes them as
The things that we've been through.
I knew there was nothing I could do
No matter how hard I tried
For this is nothing new,
But non-the-less I cried . . .
So, as sorry as I am
I want you to know
I love you and wish
It was me instead of you.

Doug
Thank you for your time in reading this. May God bless you and America!

* * *

I would like to thank those people who supported me in writing this book, long before the proof was clear to them. They believed blindly and with good faith that this story was genuine, and no matter how out of this world the events sounded, they not only defended me, but also promoted my story on their web sites.

The first person I would like to thank is Ahreeman X from the Iran Politics Club, or IPC. The website for his group the Iran Politics Club is:

http://iranpoliticsclub.net/

The forum for IPC is:

http://iranpoliticsclub.net/club/

Ahreeman is the founder of IPC, and is a member of the Qajar dynasty. He supported my initial story with one of shock, but not total disbelief. He is an Iranian exile in San Diego, California, who is also a professor at the University in San Diego. He has been helpful yet paranoid at the same time, but never disbelieving. He was the one who inspired me and urged me to write this book. He was the first person who published my book. Here is the online version of my book:

http://iranpoliticsclub.net/library/english-library/lori's-song1/index.htm

Here is the index of my writings in IPC:

http://iranpoliticsclub.net/authors/lori-forouzandeh/index.htm

I'd like to thank Debbra Kamza who has a web site that promoted her experiences with an Iranian husband and the changes she endured with him in a book called, "Lost in Foreign Passions," which is being published. She was also a big supporter of mine. "Debra also has a site that features her pictures and talent to do art as well as web design at this address, which also has already been noted but will be gladly repeated here; Debra was responsible for designing my book cover and images of this cover as well as many other pictures can be accessed at her online site at:
http://s36.photobucket.com/albums/e32/Ampbreia/ and
http://www.ampbreiareloaded.com/.

I wish to also thank Peter Khan Zendran who is a member of the Ak-konolyu dynasty, whose ancestors include Timur-I Lenk and Genghis Khan. Peter was also in close contact with the former Shah's daughter, Leila, prior to her death. Remember, nothing is what it seems, and Peter can relate to all this only too well. He has his own story to tell, but due to protective reasons, he only wants me to divulge his email address to you: peterkhanzendran@fastmail.fm.

William Beeman who also has looked into my story in Iran and is continually trying to find information that will finally someday give me some answers as to why and who was responsible for the actions done there. Bill is the head of Middle Eastern Studies at Brown University. His website is:

http://www.brown.edu/Departments/Anthropology/Beeman.html.

David Icke, who is a well known conspiracy theorist, who makes us all look at incidents a little differently and possibly in a much more sane light. Some might find him too controversial. I just find his theories fascinating. His website is: http://www.davidicke.com.

Bahman Nassiri, who has a screenplay in the works about his experiences as a spy during the revolution of 1979 in Iran. He tells of how he was inducted into the Free Masons to become a spy for Iran in England during the upheaval of the Revolution of 1979. You can read his screenplay and contact him via his website at: www.spyweb.us.

If I have missed anyone, I apologize. Just remember, there is always two sides to every story, and no two people view the same things exactly alike.

On a personal note and in closing I would like to Thank ALL OF YOU, that have taken the time to purchase this book and read it.

In doing so you not only have helped me but you have also helped those charities that I am donating funds to in order to hopefully help those that can not help themselves. I truly believe that God has a plan for all of us. It is in my opinion that even though I endured a horrific experience that will haunt me until the day I die, it is also my belief that the experience happened for a reason. Whether that reason will become known to me within my lifetime or if it will become uncovered after or upon my death I do not know. But I do know there is a reason as sure as I know there is a God. I can only do what I am capable of doing and am ready to do as my mind and soul permit. I was not ready to go forward with this book when I first wrote it, but now I am. There will be many questions and many will go unanswered since I still do not know all of the answers to this day. I don't know if I ever will have all the answers. One thing that I do know what I want to do and that is to educate people on PTSD and Bi-Polar. Two disorders that I suffer from and truly do want to become involved with not only learning more about but educating those people who are ignorant of the disorders and have misconceptions about the people around them that suffer from these disorders.

I never understood how people could judge people without knowing what was wrong with them. But we have choices and one of those choices is to LIVE LIFE OR EXIST IN IT...I CHOOSE TO LIVE IT!

THANKS FOR YOUR SUPPORT AND PEACE AND LOVE BE WITH YOU,

GOD BLESS, LORI FOROOZANDEH- www.loris-song.com

If any readers are interested in making donations to the organizations that have been most helpful to me in my times of need and hardship your generous gifts would be welcomed at:

Henry Ford Hospital
Detroit, Michigan
https://henryfordgiving.com/NetCommunity/sslpage.aspx?pid=191&srcid=191

Designate your gift to **Neurology Psychosocial Services (in the names of Andrea Thomas or Dr. Gregroy Barkley) who are continually working with PTSD patients and finding ways to help those and their problems associated with it.**
To Amnesty International
http://amnesty.org/

Brighton Hospital
http://www.brightonhospital.org/Donations/default.aspx

And to the Humane Society for those who give us unconditional love when no one else does or seem to.
http://www.hsus.org/

Printed in the United States
152874LV00002B/3/P